Using the Internet & Web sites

for beginners

Michel Dreyfus & Rob Young

WH S

WHSMITH LTD, SWINDON, WILTS. SN3 3LD
in association with:

PEARSON EDUCATION LIMITED
Head Office:
Edinburgh Gate, Harlow, Essex CM20 2JE
Tel: +44 (0)1279 623623 Fax: +44 (0)1279 431059

London Office:
128 Long Acre, London WC2E 9AN
Tel: +44 (0)20 7447 2000 Fax: +44 (0)20 7240 5771
Website: www.it-minds.com

This edition published in Great Britain 2001

British Library Cataloguing in Publication Data
A CIP catalogue record for this book can be obtained from the British Library.

ISBN 0-130-65270-9

10 9 8 7 6 5 4 3 2

Typeset by Pantek Arts Ltd, Maidstone, Kent.
Printed and bound in Great Britain by Ashford Colour Press, Gosport, Hampshire.

The publishers' policy is to use paper manufactured from sustainable forests.

contents

introduction

It's finally happened – you want to get on to the Internet! Maybe you feel as though you're arriving late at the party, and in some ways perhaps you are. But a few years ago you probably wouldn't have liked the party much: it was hard to get through the door, and there wasn't much happening when you were in.

These days there's much more going on. (You probably know a lot of people who are online already, so you don't need us to tell you that.) It's become a lot easier to join in, too. With the ever-increasing popularity of the Internet, the programs you use to sign up for an Internet account and surf the Net are actually designed for ordinary people now!

Like most things in life, the Internet is simple to use *when you know how to use it*. Because we're sure you don't want a lot of technical mumbo-jumbo, we're going to keep it simple: we'll just show you how to get connected and get on with the things you want to do – sending e-mail, browsing Web sites, and chatting with your friends.

How to use this book

If you're new to the Net, start reading from Chapter 1 to get online and learn the basics in a sensible order. But maybe you already have a connection to the Internet and you just want a bit of help with the next steps? If so, you can skip about the book all you like. You don't have to know *everything* about the Internet to use the part of it you're interested in.

Throughout the book you'll see icons in the margins. These indicate notes that provide extra detail or explain a new idea. The icon used tells you what sort of information the note contains:

This icon introduces handy shortcuts and tips such as keyboard hotkeys, expert options, and quicker ways of getting to the same place.

This icon warns you of any risks associated with a particular action, or any problems you might encounter along the way, and (where possible) shows you how to avoid them.

This icon is used to provide extra information about the topic being covered.

We're not going to try to impress you with jargon, but we can't tell you about a new subject without using a few words you haven't come across before. We'll explain them as they crop up.

What you need to know before using this book

We don't expect you to have a degree in Information Technology, but this book isn't meant to be an introduction to computers either. We're assuming that you already have a computer that runs Windows 95, 98, Millennium Edition or 2000. We're also assuming that you are fairly comfortable with the basic operation of Windows: starting programs, managing folders and files, using the mouse, and so on.

Along with a computer, you must also have a telephone line. There's nothing special about this phone line, but it's the vital link between your computer and the Internet so it's not an optional extra. (We'll look at how these things are linked together in Chapter 3.)

Do I need a powerful computer?

Yes and no. It all depends on your patience...and your budget.

Processor and memory

If you get a taste for some of the Internet's multimedia content (movies, animations, virtual reality, video phone calls), a reasonably powerful computer is important – a Pentium II or later with at least 32Mb RAM. If you could still buy such a computer today, of course, it would be at an almost giveaway price, so the Internet doesn't demand a particularly expensive PC. If you're not interested in the multimedia aspects, an old Pentium PC with 16Mb RAM would just about do the job.

Hard disk

You will need to install some new programs to access the Internet, and you will probably collect other files on your travels. At the beginning, like somebody who starts working in a pastry shop, you will want to stuff yourself with everything you see and this information is quickly going to fill up your hard disk. Text doesn't take up much space, but anything to do with multimedia (sounds, pictures, animations, movies) is disk-hungry. Nowadays, a basic hard disk is rarely less than eight gigabytes. You should allow at least 200 megabytes (Mb) for the new software and the other bits and pieces that you will no doubt collect.

Screen

First and foremost, you need a colour monitor. You've almost certainly got one, but if you haven't they can be bought very cheaply. A 15-inch screen is a comfortable size for occasional use, but for any regular computer use (not just the Internet) a 17-inch screen is preferable.

There are two aspects to the way your screen is set up: the number of colours it can display, and the resolution (the number of dots used to make up the whole picture). A minimum setting is 256 colours at a resolution of 800 × 600; a better setting is 65,536 colours (known as High Colour) at 1024 × 768. You can adjust these settings using the **Display** option in the Windows Control Panel.

Modem

The modem is another important piece of equipment, the item which connects your computer to the telephone line. This topic is important enough to warrant more than a passing reference, and we will return to it in Chapter 3.

A last word before you start

Nothing moves as fast as the world of the Internet. It's built by real people like you and me, and whenever they feel like it they can change what they put there, or rename it, or remove it.

We've included screenshots of a lot of Internet sites in this book, and mentioned a lot of site addresses. Although we checked them all at the time of going to print, we can't guarantee that they will still be correct when you use them. That's the Internet for you – it never stands still!

1

What is the Internet?

- How does the Internet work?
- Internet resources
- Internet security

If you're new to the Internet it must seem a bit strange. You've probably heard people mention e-mail, the World Wide Web, chat rooms, and so on, and you may have at least a vague idea what those things are. But most beginners have questions like '*Can I get the Internet on CD to save the cost of the phone calls?*' or '*Can I send flowers by e-mail?*', so let's start with a quick look at what the Internet actually is and what you can use it for.

> **+info**
> *A network is two or more computers connected together so that information on one machine can be shared/accessed by the other. Users on either machine can also decide for themselves what information is shared and what should remain private. They may also protect information with a password so that only users who know the password can access that information.*

How does the Internet work?

The Internet is a vast computer network. Small networks are connected by running cables between the computers, and that's fine for machines that are all in the same office or building, but in a larger network (particularly a worldwide network like the Internet), cabling all those computers together wouldn't be a popular option!

That could have been a major stumbling block in the creation of the Internet, but fortunately all the cables were in place already: they were attached to telephones! We could just pick up a phone in our home or office and those cables could connect us to another telephone on the other side of the world. If it worked for phones, why not let computers talk to each other along the same cables?

And that's how the Internet works. There were a couple of problems to solve, though. First, computers don't talk, of course – when computer information moves around, it does so silently – but telephone cables transfer *sound*. To solve this problem, a new gadget called a **modem** was connected to the computers. This converted the information into sound and sent it down the telephone line; at the other end, another modem attached to the other computer converted the sound back to data.

Internet resources

So everything you can find on the Internet exists in the form of computer data. This data is spread about over hundreds of thousands of computers around the world. These computers perform different *services* – some, for example, deal with handling e-mail *messages*; others help you chat to friends; more let you look at pages on the World Wide Web. Some Internet-related services are more popular (and more useful) than others, and you'll probably end up using the same two or three most of the time. Here's a quick look at the four most popular Internet services.

E-mail

This is electronic mail, commonly called by its abbreviation *e-mail*. Your credibility will grow no end if, on your business card, under your name and occupation, you can put yourname@yourcompany.co.uk. Using e-mail you can send a message to someone in any part of the world extremely quickly (most messages arrive in a matter of minutes).

E-mail is the most used of the various Internet services: it may not be the most glamorous, but it's quick, easy, and extremely useful. However, the volume of e-mail traffic on the Net represents less than 10% of the total amount of traffic whizzing around. This is because an e-mail message is a tiny amount of data compared with some of the other uses of the Net (Web pages, sound and video, for instance).

Figure 1.1 shows what an e-mail message looks like in a program called Outlook Express. This is the most popular of the many e-mail programs available, chiefly because it's included with the Microsoft Windows operating system.

There are also e-mail-based services known as **mailing lists**. Instead of writing to an individual, you send your message to the list and the message is then sent to all the people on that list.

The World Wide Web

The World Wide Web (often referred to just as 'the Web') is one of the most recent Internet services to appear, and it's the one that has really caught the public imagination. So much so, in fact, that many beginners believe the Web *is* the Internet.

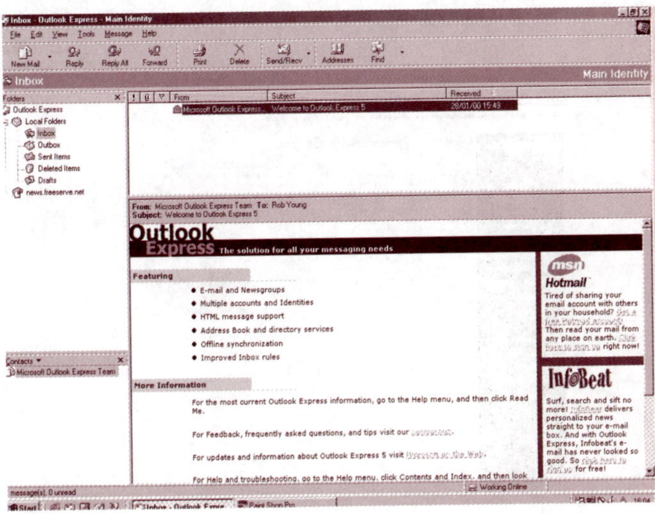

Figure 1.1

Outlook Express, the most popular e-mail program.

Its advantage is that it presents all sorts of information – scientific, technical, political, administrative, humorous, and so on – in a very attractive form (with pictures, sound, and animations for instance). Through a virtual link system called **hypertext**, it allows the surfer to move from one page to another with a single mouse click. The pages may be on different computers, and those computers may be on different continents, but the system hides all that from you. As an example, Figure 1.2 shows the main page (or *home page* as it's known) of a Web site called Castles Unlimited.

Among the various services offered by the Web, there are two which have quickly become very important: electronic commerce (otherwise known as **e-commerce**) and search engines (which we'll come to in Chapter 7), which allow you to find information on almost any subject.

+info

*A **Web site** is a term used to describe a set of related pages on the Web: all the pages are related and written by the same person or organisation (in the same way that a set of chapters is known as a book).*

Newsgroups

This is an electronic mail system very similar to mailing lists, mentioned above, but with a different structure. There are over 50,000 groups, each of which has its own name and deals with

Figure 1.2

The home page of the Castles Unlimited Web site.

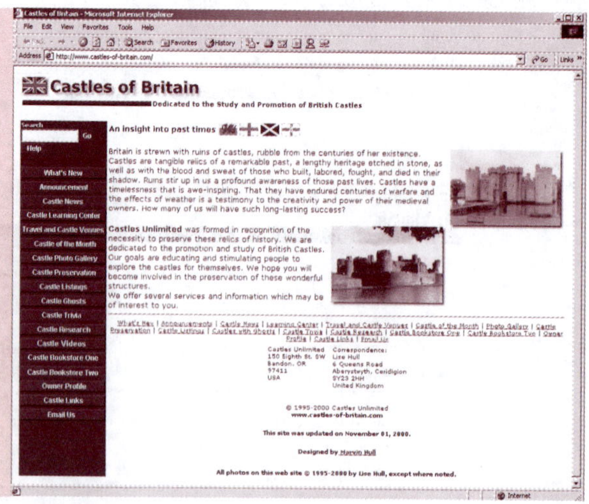

a particular subject. Anyone with an interest in a certain subject can subscribe to one of the groups that deals with it, contribute their own messages and read messages left by others.

Chat

On the Internet, the word 'chatting' doesn't mean verbal chat (although that's possible too if you have a microphone plugged into your computer's soundcard). Instead it means typing messages back and forth to hold a conversation, and those short messages are sent almost instantly to everyone else taking part (perhaps one person or a whole group). Everyone taking part has a small window where the entire conversation is displayed, and a second small window where you type what you want to 'say' and press **Enter** to send it.

Internet security

There are certainly risks in using the Net that you wouldn't expect, and from time to time people do get caught out by them. But there are other things that most users (if they stopped to think about it for a moment) would realise were stupidly risky.

Unfortunately, the Net can sometimes lull you into a false sense of security: after all, you're comfortable and warm, and sitting safely in front of your computer. What could possibly go wrong? In this section we'll point out some of the pitfalls to be aware of when using the Internet.

Keeping children safe

The Internet has its fair share of sex and smut, just as it has motoring, cookery, sports, films, and so on. We won't pretend that your kids *can't* come into contact with explicit images and language, but there are two important points to note. First, you're no more likely to stumble upon pornography while looking for a sports site than you are to stumble upon film reviews or recipes. If you want to find that sort of content, you have to go looking for it. Second, most of the sexually explicit sites on the World Wide Web are *private* – to get inside you need a credit card. Nevertheless, there *are* dangers on the Net, and given unrestricted freedom, your kids may come into contact with unsuitable material.

However, these are not good reasons to deny children access to the Internet. Quite simply, the Internet is a fact of life that isn't going to go away, and will feature more strongly in our children's lives than it does in ours. More and more schools are recognising this, and promoting use of the Internet in homework and class projects. The wealth of web sites created by and for children is a great indicator of their active participation in the growth of the Net. Rather than depriving children of this incredible resource, agree a few ground rules at the outset: when they can surf, why they should never give out their address, school name or telephone number, what sort of sites they can visit, and what to do if they receive messages that make them uncomfortable. For some excellent practical advice on this subject, all parents should visit Yahooligans at http://www.yahooligans.com/docs/safety.

If you're ever concerned about the web sites your children might be visiting, remember that you can open Internet Explorer's History panel to see a list of recently accessed sites sorted by week and day.

You can also install a 'babysitter' program that can limit the amount of time children spend online, prevent them from accessing certain sites, and monitor the sites they do visit. Two popular programs are Cyber Patrol from http://www.cyberpatrol.com and Net Nanny from http://www.netnanny.com.

Shopping online

A popular myth about the Internet is that credit-card transactions are risky because your card number can be stolen. To put this in perspective, consider how you use your credit or debit card in the 'real world'. How many people get to see your card number during a normal week? How much time does your card spend out of your view when you use it? The truth is, card numbers are easy to steal. It takes a lot more effort and technical know-how to steal numbers on the Internet.

Making the computer hacker's job more difficult in this department, modern browsers now encrypt the data they send, and most of the web sites at which you can use your credit card run on **secure servers** that have their own built-in encryption. So when you visit one of these secure sites, enter your card number and click the button to send it, your number will appear as meaningless gibberish to anyone managing to hack into the system. In fact, credit card companies actually regard online transactions as being the *safest* kind.

+info

*It's easy to recognise a secure site in Internet Explorer: look for a little padlock symbol in the lower right corner of the browser. You'll also notice that the **http://** in the address bar changes to **https://**. More and more shopping sites are becoming secure all the time, and those that aren't usually offer alternative payment methods.*

Viruses

Viruses can't find their way onto your computer during ordinary Net surfing – you're not taking a greater risk by surfing for two hours a day than only surfing for one. But you might receive a virus-infected program on a floppy disk or CD-ROM, in an e-mail message, or by downloading it from the Internet. In almost all cases, your computer can only become infected by that virus when you run the program, so always use a virus-checker to scan software received by one of these methods before running it. Two of the best-known virus-checker programs can be found at http://www.mcafee.com and http://www.symantec.com.

An increasingly popular type of virus is the so-called 'e-mail virus'. An ordinary e-mail message is just plain text, making it completely harmless, but you can receive programs as e-mail attachments which definitely *could* be infected with a virus. Always save e-mail attachments and virus-check them before opening them.

Although you should always be suspicious of attachments from people you don't know, remember that viruses can come from friends and colleagues too: they may be unaware that their system is infected when they send you an attachment. Many recent types of virus automatically copy themselves to everyone in your e-mail address book, so nowadays you're actually more likely to receive infected attachments from someone you know than from someone you don't!

A final type of virus risk comes from malicious scripts built into HTML e-mail. Outlook Express supports this type of e-mail, and with so many Outlook Express users out there it's an attractive target for virus writers. To guard against viruses in HTML e-mail, follow these two steps:

1 In Outlook Express, go to **Tools/Options/Security**, select the option labelled **Restricted sites zone** and click **OK**.
2 In Control Panel, run the Internet Options applet, and choose the Security tab. Select the **Restricted sites** icon at the top of the page, drag the slider below up to **High** (if it's not there already), and click **OK**.

2

Connecting to the Internet

- **Connection options**
- **What do the connection calls cost?**
- **Free Internet access**
- **How to choose your Internet Service Provider**
- **Internet Service Providers in the UK**

Before you can use any of the Internet's services, you need to 'get connected'. The majority of Internet users don't have their computers permanently connected to the Internet: although it's possible, it isn't necessary and it would cost thousands of pounds per year. Instead, most users set up an account with a company that *does* have a permanent connection. These companies are known as **Internet Service Providers** (ISPs). Whenever you want to use the Internet, your computer will connect to your ISP's computer using your telephone line, and will be connected to the Internet through theirs while you surf the Web, send and receive e-mail, and so on. In this chapter we'll look at how to connect, along with what it's going to cost (if anything!).

Connection options

We've already established that you'll connect through an Internet Service Provider, or **ISP**. In the UK, there are several hundred service providers ranging from large companies like Demon Internet, Freeserve, BT Internet and America Online (AOL), all serving many thousands of subscribers, to regional providers with far fewer subscribers.

The simplest and most widespread way to get online is to choose a service provider and connect using a modem and an ordinary telephone line. British Telecom also offers the option of connecting via faster digital lines by purchasing a package it calls **Home Highway**. In this case, instead of a modem you'll use a device called a **terminal adapter**. Most service providers will let you connect using either method, but (as you'd expect) you'll pay a little extra for the faster option. Let's take a look at both.

Standard telephone line

The advantage of normal telephone lines is that they are easily available and they don't cost the earth. Apart from the cost of going online, which we'll look at later in this chapter, what you're mainly concerned with at this stage is how fast the information can reach you from the Internet.

The speed is variable: it can depend upon which ISP you set up your account with, how busy the Internet is while you're online, how popular the Web site is that you're visiting, and several other factors. Mostly, though, the speed depends upon your modem. Modern modems have a theoretical maximum speed of 56,000 bps (*bits per second*), although you'll never quite squeeze this much speed out of them. The quality of ordinary telephone lines means that your modem will never manage a speed of more than 50,000 bps.

Using a telephone line to connect to the Internet creates the same problems as using the family TV as a computer screen: only one person can use it at any one time. Be prepared for family upheavals if you're blocking access to the one-and-only telephone line when you surf the Net! There are two possible solutions: one is to get a second telephone line installed especially for Internet use; the second, which we'll look at now, is to upgrade to a Home Highway line.

Home Highway line

This is a British Telecom package aimed at home Internet users, although it's also available to businesses. Your normal telephone wall-box is replaced with a larger box, and you'll gain two extra phone numbers. You'll also need to replace your modem with a terminal adapter, mentioned above, or an ISDN card: these are effectively the same thing, but the first is an external unit that plugs into your computer and the second installs inside your computer.

> **+info**
>
> *Along with the convenience of Home Highway, you also get increased speed. Internet connections will be at 64,000 bps and, unlike the humble modem, this is a guaranteed speed. It's also possible to combine the two digital lines to connect to the Net at 128,000 bps, although currently few ISPs allow you to do this.*

With these hardware changes made, you can now connect up to two digital devices (such as two computers) and two analogue devices (such as a phone and a fax machine) to the junction box. Best of all, you can use two of these devices at the same time. So you can hold two telephone conversations, or talk to someone while sending someone else a fax, or (as we're concerned with here) surf the Net while making or taking phone calls.

ADSL

ADSL (*Asymmetric Digital Subscriber Line*) is another recent arrival on the communications scene, and as of mid-2001 it's available in only a few of the UK's major cities. Unlike an ordinary telephone line or Home Highway, with ADSL your computer is permanently

> *The 'A' in ADSL for 'Asymmetric' is important: it means that information you send doesn't travel at the same speed as information you receive.*
>
> *When sending information from your computer, the speed drops to 256,000 bps.*

connected to the Internet. BT is offering a range of ADSL packages under the brand name **BTopenworld**, and these should soon also become available (under different names) through service providers such as Virgin Net and AOL. The speed of an ADSL connection will be at least 512,000 bps (roughly ten times the top speed of a modem connection), with speeds of up to 2 Mbits per second (four times as fast) available at an increased price.

What do the connection calls cost?

If you opt for the ordinary phone line or Home Highway method of connecting to the Internet, the connection is made using your phone line. And although it's not your telephone making the call, the pricing is exactly the same. Once again, there are two variables that affect the cost of the calls: what time you go online, and what number your computer has to dial.

- **Dial-up number**: When you choose your service provider, they should give you a local-rate dial-up number for your computer to call. This may be an 0845 number, or it may be a number with a local STD code. Large national ISPs usually use 0845 numbers. Don't choose a small ISP based in another part of the country unless they also give you a local-rate number or you'll be paying far higher call charges than you need to!
- **Dial-up time**: Telephone charges vary according to time of day. British Telecom's charges at the time of writing are 4p per minute daytime; 1.5p per minute evenings; and 1p per minute at weekends.

Premier Line

In return for a membership fee which can be paid monthly or annually, you receive a 15% discount off direct dialled local, regional, national and international calls if your quarterly phone bill is high enough to qualify for the scheme.

Friends & Family

Free to join, this scheme gives a 10% discount on calls to 10 selected numbers, and a 20% discount on calls to one particular number (your 'BestFriend'). Your selection can include one international and one mobile number.

> **+info**
>
> *This may soon be academic. Many ISPs are trying to provide what's known as 'unmetered access', meaning that you pay a single fixed annual fee for your Internet calls rather than a per-minute charge, and even the telephone companies are slowly edging towards the holy grail of free local calls.*

SurfTime

This BT option can make the Internet more affordable by charging a single monthly rate for your connection calls, no matter how long you spend online (known as *unmetered access*). Direct from BT, the SurfTime option costs £20 per month for unlimited surfing all day long, or £5 for evenings and weekends only. The same option can be bought through a number of ISPs such as BTclick, Virgin Net and Freeserve.

> *It's highly recommended that you make your Internet dial-up number your 'BestFriend' in your Friends & Family list. You'll probably spend more time per quarter connected to this number than talking to one particular friend or family member.*

Free Internet access

Many ISPs now provide a free service. At the time of writing, 'free' means that you only pay for your connection calls (covered on previous pages). The benefits of signing up with a free ISP are twofold:

- If you're not satisfied with the service you simply stop using it: you're not paying, so you don't need to cancel.
- If you hear of a service that sounds better, you can try it alongside your existing account. With no charges to pay, it's easy to 'audition' a service in this way, and you might even decide to keep using both.

What we'd really like 'free' to mean is that even the cost of the calls is free, and this type of free connection is gradually becoming available. Along with the SurfTime package mentioned above, BT is slowly edging towards making local calls entirely free, and the huge Internet service America Online has introduced its own form of unmetered access for its subscribers.

There are two catches with free access that you should be aware of. The first (and it's not a major catch) is that you have to pay a massive price for phone calls to the company's support staff if you get into difficulties: most companies charge between 50p and £1 per minute. Fortunately, though, you shouldn't get into difficulties very often, and you'll probably never need to phone that support line.

> **+info**
> *Companies can afford to provide free access to the Internet because instead of taking their money directly from you, they take a percentage of the cost of your connection call from BT and sell advertising on the Web sites.*

The second catch is that (at the moment) you get what you pay for. Many users of free services find that they can't connect at certain times of day, or the service is slow, or otherwise unreliable. If you're paying for access, the quality of service is currently much more likely to be high, and the company will make more effort to keep you as a customer.

How to choose your Internet Service Provider

In choosing an Internet Service Provider, you care about two things: *What do they charge?* and *Are they any good?* If you've decided to go for a free service provider (and that's the recommended place to start for beginners) the first question can be skipped, of course. If you prefer to pay for Internet access, a standard charge is about £10–15 per month plus VAT.

The second question involves rather a lot of different things, so let's go through them one by one. At the end of this chapter, you'll find a list of some of the best-known ISPs in the UK.

User support

You need to know whether the company in question has a support phone line, when it's available, and whether calls to the support line are charged at a premium rate. In general, free services charge for their support line, and pay-for services don't. Needless to say, if support won't be available when you're most likely to be trying to use the Internet, it doesn't matter what it costs!

Points of presence

A Point of Presence (or *PoP*) is a connection point your computer dials into to connect to the Internet. Large service providers have PoPs throughout the country, but smaller providers may have PoPs only in their own county or town. If you live in the same town, that's fine. But if you live miles away you may be paying for a national-rate phone call to connect rather than a local-rate call. Make sure the ISP you choose either has a local PoP or allows you to connect through an 0845 (or equivalent local-rate) phone number.

Number of modems

Some companies are a bit coy about publicising their modem-to-subscriber ratio (and they may not always stick to it) but it's useful information to check if you're planning to pay for your Internet access. The more modems the company has per subscriber, the better your chances of not getting an engaged tone when you try to connect to the Internet. A ratio of about 1:12 is reckoned to be average, meaning that one in twelve subscribers can be online at the same time.

Free Web space allocated

Most ISPs include some **Web space** in their subscriptions. If you decide to build your own Web site, this is where your site will be stored so that the rest of the online world can see it. The amount of space provided varies enormously: some providers still offer only 2Mb Web space while others offer 50Mb! For most non-business sites, 5–10Mb is quite enough space.

Usenet newsgroup access

Does your chosen ISP offer newsgroup access? Usually the answer is 'yes', but a very few don't. How many newsgroups do they offer? There are over 50,000 in existence, and most ISPs won't offer all of them, but you should expect to be able to access at least 50% of them. Does the ISP offer its own groups? These allow subscribers of the same service to communicate with each other, and this could be helpful if you have problems and can't get through to (or afford!) the support line.

Number of mailboxes offered

If somebody else is going to share your Internet access, it's better if your e-mail messages don't get mixed up with theirs. Most service providers offer five or more different names with one subscription, so that you can each have different e-mail addresses.

Choice of username and password

Your **username** is a unique name that identifies you to your chosen service provider. When you sign up, you can usually choose your username (a combination of numbers, letters, dots, hyphens and underscore characters, but no spaces). You will also be assigned a **password**. Keep your username and password secret, and make sure you don't forget them!

Internet Service Providers in the UK

The following is a short list of Internet Service Providers. If you already have Internet access you can find out more about these services by visiting their Web sites or sending them an e-mail message. In some cases you may be able to sign up for a new account at the Web site. If you're new to the Internet, pick up the phone and give the service a call to find out more about them. Many services will be happy to send you everything you need on a CD-ROM; others may direct you to a High Street store to pick up a free sign-up CD.

Company:	America Online (AOL)
Telephone:	0800 279 1234
E-mail:	queryuk@aol.com
Web site:	www.aol.com

Notes: 10Mb Web space, 7 e-mail addresses, single monthly fee with unmetered access and no call charges.

Company:	BT Internet
Telephone:	0800 800001
E-mail:	support@btinternet.com
Web site:	www.btinternet.com

Notes: Unlimited Web space and e-mail addresses. Free weekend and evening calls via BT SurfTime.

Company:	ClaraNET Ltd
Telephone:	0800 358 2828
E-mail:	sales@clara.net
Web site:	www.clara.net

Notes: Various account offers, reduced call charges.

Company:	CompuServe (CSi)
Telephone:	0870 6000 800
E-mail:	UKCSSVC@cs.com
Web site:	www.compuserve.co.uk

Notes: 10Mb Web space, 7 e-mail addresses, phone for software or download.

Company:	Free-Online
Telephone:	0870 7060504
E-mail:	sales@free-online.net
Web site:	www.free-online.net

Notes: Unlimited Web space and e-mail addresses, free support.

Company: Freeserve
Telephone: 0870 872 0099
E-mail: info@freeserve.com
Web site: www.freeserve.com

Notes: Free disk from Dixons or PC World, or sign up online. 15Mb Web space, unlimited e-mail addresses. Unlimited free evening and weekend access calls via BT SurfTime.

Company: ic24
Telephone: 020 7643 3215
E-mail: ic24@mgn.co.uk
Web site: www.ic24.net

Notes: Phone for software or download. 10Mb Web space, 5 e-mail addresses. Limited free access call time at weekends.

Company: LineOne
Telephone: 0800 111 210
E-mail: support@lineone.net
Web site: www.lineone.net

Notes: 5 e-mail addresses, Web space, sign up online.

Company: UUNET
Telephone: 0500 474739
E-mail: sales@uk.uu.net
Web site: www.uk.uu.net

Notes: 50Mb Web space, 5 e-mail addresses.

Company: Virgin Net
Telephone: 0500 558800
E-mail: advice@virgin.net
Web site: www.virgin.net

Notes: Sign up online. 10Mb Web space, 5 e-mail addresses. Free evening and weekend access calls via BT SurfTime.

Company: Zetnet Services
Telephone: 01595 696667
E-mail: info@zetnet.co.uk
Web site: www.zetnet.co.uk

Notes: 25Mb Web space, unlimited e-mail addresses.

3

Your first connection

- **Modem installation**
- **Software installation**
- **Using your connection**

Some people say that installing an Internet connection on a computer is difficult. A few years ago this would have been true, but these days it's usually as straightforward as installing any other piece of software: you just insert the CD-ROM, follow the on-screen instructions, and away you go.

There are two reasons for this. First, most new computers come with a modem already installed, so that's something you won't have to do yourself. Second, recent versions of Windows include complete support for Internet connections, along with most of the software you'll use when you're on the Net.

When you sign up for an account with a service provider, they'll almost certainly give you a CD-ROM and a very short page of instructions, and you'll be online in minutes. You can then skip to the last pages of this chapter, *Using your connection*. It's useful to know how to set up a connection manually, though, in case something goes wrong, and this is what the first part of this chapter is all about.

Modem installation

There are two types of modems: *internal* modems, inserted into a PCI slot inside the computer, and *external* modems, small boxes linked by a cable to the computer's serial port (also known as a COM port, short for 'communications') or USB socket.

Although it costs a little more, the external variety has several benefits:

- You can use it with another computer whose internal connectors may be different.
- Its installation is easier: just plug it in and connect the serial or USB cable.
- It has warning lights which provide information on what's happening during your connection.

The current price of a modem varies between £25 and £100+, according to its technical specifications and the gadgets it comes equipped with. Modems usually come with a floppy disk containing a variety of software such as fax programs. The majority of modems are Plug-and-Play-compatible, so installation is extremely easy and all the cables you need will be included with your modem.

Software installation

There are several pieces of software that need installing before you can connect to the Internet:

- The modem driver, which allows your computer to communicate with your modem once the two have been connected. (If you change your modem, you need to uninstall the old driver and install the driver for the new one.) This will be one of the items supplied on the floppy disk accompanying the modem.
- Dial-Up Networking, the software which will manage the TCP/IP (see end of chapter) connection used by all Internet resources. This is included with Windows 95 and later, and is probably

already installed on your computer: if it is, you'll see a folder named **Dial-Up Networking** when you double-click your My Computer icon.

- Connection to the specific Internet Provider with which you have taken up a subscription. You need to create such a connection for each ISP you've signed up with (probably only one so far).
- A **Web browser** to access Web sites.
- An e-mail program to send and receive e-mail messages.

As you'll learn in the next couple of chapters, Windows provides the last two items in the list so you probably have these already. If you don't, they are both freely available on almost any Internet-related magazine cover-disk.

The modem driver

When you installed Windows, if you have an external modem, it is possible that the modem was not switched on. In this case it could not be recognised and you need to install it. Start by checking the modem link to the computer and switch it on. Then restart your computer. When it starts running, Windows will know that there is something new in your computer and will prompt you to proceed with the installation of the software. But you can also follow these instructions, without restarting your computer:

1. Click on **Start/Settings/Control Panel**.
2. In the Control Panel window, double-click the **Modems** icon.
3. On the General tab, click on **Add**. The Hardware Wizard displays its first page. Don't tick the check box in front of 'Do not detect modem'.
4. Click on **Next** and Windows will search for your modem.
5. If, in the next window, you see that the type of modem recognised is 'Standard Modem', this means that Windows has found your modem but cannot tell which brand of modem it is. In this case, click on the **Modify** button.

6 The next page will display two list-boxes, as you can see in Figure 3.1. In the left one you'll see the names of modem brands: pick the brand that matches your modem. Then, in the right window, choose your modem type. These indications are usually to be found on its front. Then click on the **Next** button.

If you can't find your modem in these lists, you need to use the drivers on the floppy disk which comes with your modem by clicking on the **Have Disk** button and following the indications provided by the Wizard.

7 A final window prompts you to click on the **Finish** button.

8 The Modems Properties page is displayed with your modem shown in the list of installed devices (Figure 3.2). To check that Windows can communicate with your modem properly, click on the **Diagnostics** tab and on the port used by the modem (usually COM2), then click on the **More Info** button.

9 Within a few seconds, if everything works as it should, you should see the window filling with mysterious codes. Don't worry about what they mean: for our purposes, they just mean everything works!

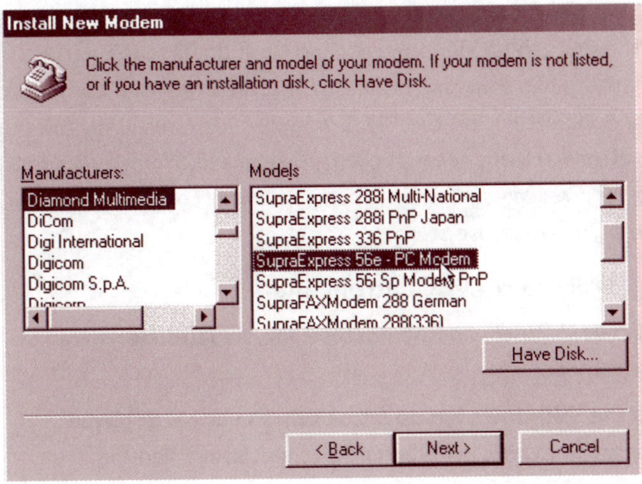

Figure 3.1

Choose your modem from the dual lists in the Install New Modem dialogue box.

Figure 3.2

After completing the Install New Modem Wizard, your modem will appear on the Modems Properties page.

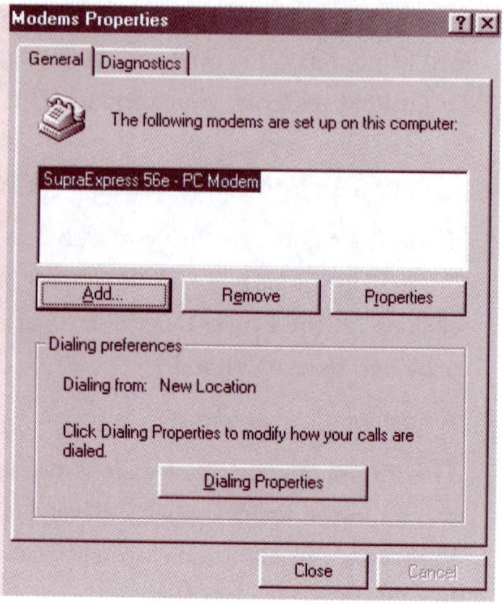

Dial-Up Networking

To connect to an ISP through a telephone line, you use a connection protocol known as PPP (*Point to Point Protocol*). For this you will need to use software called a *TCP/IP stack*, because TCP/IP is the connection protocol used on the Internet.

Windows 95, 98, Millennium Edition and 2000 come with all the software you need to connect to a network, as do modern Apple Macs like the iMac. With Windows 95 and later, the first thing to do is to see whether that software is already installed on your computer. To do this, double-click on the My Computer icon and look for the **Dial-Up Networking** icon shown in Figure 3.3. If you can, go straight to the *Creating and configuring a new connection* section below.

Otherwise, follow these steps:

1 Click on **Start/Settings/Control Panel**.

2 In the Control Panel window, double-click the **Add/Remove Programs** icon.

3 Click on the **Windows Setup** tab. A dialogue box is displayed which tells you to wait while Setup searches for installed components. After a few seconds, the list of components is displayed.

4 Find the **Communications** item in this window and click on it.

Figure 3.3

The Dial-up Networking icon shows that Windows' Internet connection software is already installed.

5 Click on the **Details** button. In the Communications window which appears (shown in Figure 3.4), tick the box beside **Dial-Up Networking** and click **OK** to close the Communications window.

6 Click on **OK** in the main dialogue box. If the Windows CD-ROM is not in the appropriate drive, you will be asked to insert it. The required files will be installed on your computer, which takes just a few seconds, and a dialogue box will then prompt you to restart your computer.

Creating and configuring a connection

There are two ways of creating a connection: either by using a connection CD-ROM which your service provider sends you (or which you find bundled with a computer magazine), or by following the various steps required under Windows if your Internet Provider has simply given you the essential details. Once again, most ISPs will give you a CD-ROM that does everything for you, but here's what to do if you find yourself faced with using the second method.

What you need to know

Before starting to install a new connection, make sure that your Internet Provider has given you the following details:

Figure 3.4

Installing Dial-Up Networking from the Windows CD-ROM.

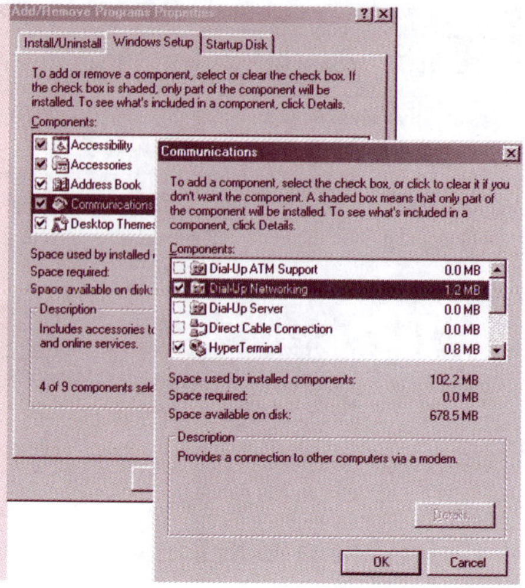

- The dial-up telephone number to connect to the Internet;
- Your username and password;
- Your ISP's primary Domain Name System (DNS) address (and, perhaps, a secondary DNS);
- The name of its mail server (usually something like mail.serviceprovider .co.uk);
- The name of its news server (usually news.serviceprovider.co.uk).

> ! *Your password might be chosen by you or may have been assigned to you by your service provider. What matters is that you know it (and can remember it) – without it you can't go online!*

Creating a connection

Open My Computer by double-clicking its icon and then double-click on the **Dial-Up Networking** icon. A new window opens, with a single icon labelled **Make New Connection** (Figure 3.5).

Double-click this icon to launch the Make New Connection wizard which will take you through the following steps:

1 The first window prompts you to name this connection as 'My Connection', which isn't particularly imaginative, so you'll probably want to choose something different. Then click on the **Next** button.

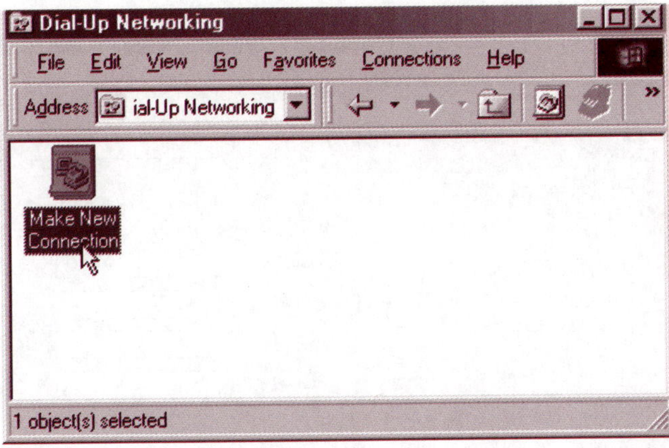

Figure 3.5
Double-click this icon to launch the Make New Connection Wizard.

2 In the next window, you will need to enter the Area code in the appropriate box. In the Telephone number box, enter your ISP's dial-up number (with or without spaces – they'll be ignored if you include them) and keep the Country code as it is. Then click on the **Next** button.

3 The third window summarises what you've just done. Click **Finish** to confirm.

> **+info**
> *The connection name is entirely for your own use. You can pick any name at all here to give the icon a name you'll recognise in future.*

When you finish, you'll be returned to the Dial-Up Networking folder where you should see a new icon with the name you chose in Step 1 above. Later you'll be able to double-click this to go online. First, though, there are a few more steps to take care of.

Configuring your connection

To configure the connection you've just created, you need to modify its properties.

1 Right-click the new icon and choose **Properties** from the context menu that appears.

> *To make this connection icon more easily accessible when you want to go online, use the right mouse button to drag it onto the desktop and choose **Create Shortcut(s) Here** when prompted.*

Figure 3.6

The Server Types and TCP/IP Settings pages after modifying them. (Your DNS settings will be different from those shown here.)

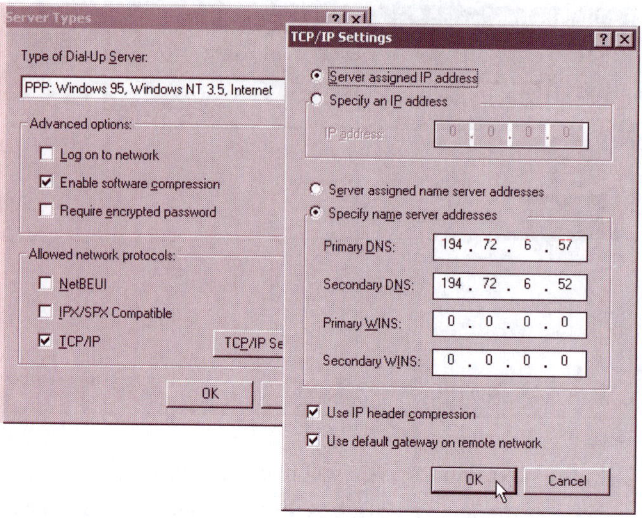

2 Select the Server Types tab, and remove the check marks from most of the boxes on the page so that the only checked items are:

- Enable software compression;
- TCP/IP.

3 If your ISP gave you a primary (and perhaps a secondary) DNS address, click the **TCP/IP Settings** button. Make sure the button beside **Specify name server addresses** is selected, and type your Primary and Secondary DNS addresses into the appropriate boxes (Figure 3.6).

4 Click **OK** in all the open dialogue boxes to confirm the changes you've made and close them.

Using your connection

That's it! Now you're ready to go online, so you need to grab the two pieces of information we haven't yet used: your username and password. Double-click your connection icon in the Dial-Up Networking folder (or the shortcut to it on your desktop, if you followed the note above) and you'll see a dialogue box like the one in the screenshot below. Windows will probably have a guess at your username, but it probably won't get it right; the password field will be blank when the dialogue box appears. Type the correct username and the password (which will be automatically masked with asterisks to prevent anyone else in the room reading it from your screen) and click the **Connect** button (Figure 3.7).

You'll hear your modem squeaking and squawking for about 20 seconds (unless you have Home Highway, which is silent) and a dialogue should then inform you that you're connected. You'll also see a tiny icon beside the clock at the bottom-right of your screen which flashes to indicate data passing backwards and forwards from the Internet to your computer.

To be absolutely sure that everything is OK, try visiting a Web site. Launch Internet Explorer by clicking on its icon to the right of the Start button, in the Windows taskbar (a blue 'e'). Near the top of the Internet Explorer window you'll see a wide text field labelled **Address**. Click in that field and type www.yahoo.co.uk, then press **Enter**. This is the address of the famous Yahoo! Web site, and within a few seconds you should see the home page of this site appear.

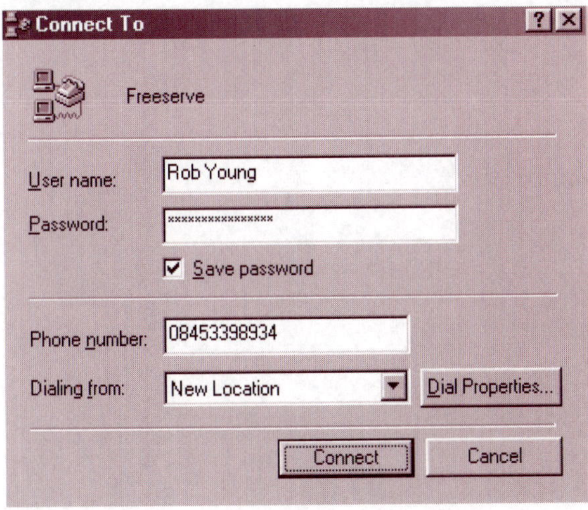

Figure 3.7

Enter your username and password, and you're ready to connect.

So now you're connected, *and* you've visited your first Web site. In Chapter 4 we'll take a closer look at the World Wide Web and the Internet Explorer browser.

In the meantime, though, how do you *disconnect* from the Internet? Just double-click that tiny flashing icon beside the clock. A dialogue box will appear giving you some information about how long you've been online and how much data has been sent and received by your computer. You'll also see a button labelled **Disconnect**: click that and your modem will hang up the line (the same as putting the phone down if you'd been making an ordinary telephone call).

Notes

TCP/IP (Transmission Control Protocol/Internet Protocol) – two vital protocols that work together to handle communications between your computer and the rest of the Internet.

4

Browsing the World Wide Web

- Web addresses
- Installing Internet Explorer
- Installing Netscape Navigator
- Installing Opera
- Getting started on the Web

The World Wide Web is so popular that it's often confused with the Internet itself, although in fact it's just one of the Internet's many resources. There are two reasons why the Web has become so widely used. First, it's extremely easy to use (or, more accurately, the software you use to look at Web sites is easy to use); second, it's a true multimedia environment: Web pages can contain text, images, animations, movies, interactive content, small programs, and lots more.

The program you use to access this lot is called a **Web browser** (usually shortened to *browser*). The browser is the most important piece of Internet software you'll have (apart from your e-mail program, perhaps, as we'll see in Chapter 5) since it allows you to do almost everything you need to do on the Net. In this chapter, we'll learn how to surf the Web and how to use your browser.

Web addresses

The most important aspect of the Web is that it uses a technology called **hypertext** to let you jump from one page (or *resource*) to another with just one mouse-click. You might have seen similar systems at work in Windows Help files, Apple Hypercard, or multimedia encyclopaedias on CD-ROMs.

Hypertext is a more advanced system than any of these, since it allows that one simple mouse-click to open pages or files on any Internet-connected computer in the world: all the complicated stuff is hidden from view. To make this work, each resource has its own unique address known as a **URL** (Uniform Resource Locator). It's useful to understand how a URL is put together, so let's take an example and pull it apart. Here's a URL which could be a single Web page on a company's Web site:

> **+info**
>
> *If you're a Windows user, you'll notice that Internet addresses use forward slashes (/) rather than the backslashes you're more used to (\).*

http://www.city1.co.uk/design/pages/index.htm

This is made up of the following:

> **+info**
>
> *The extension for Web pages can also be **.html**. You will come across a few other file extensions which display something that looks a lot like a Web page, such as **.asp** and **.cfm**.*

- The **http://** prefix, which indicates that this is a resource on the World Wide Web.
- A server address: www.city1.co.uk/ – most Web servers have a name beginning with www. In this case, the **.co.uk** shows that the server is in the United Kingdom.
- The path **design/pages/** shows which directory on the server's hard disk contains the file we want.
- The file name **index.htm**. The extension **.htm** indicates that the file is a Web page, but files of any type can be placed on a Web server (just as you can place any type of file on your own hard disk).

Installing Internet Explorer

If you use Windows 98, 2000 or Millennium Edition, there is nothing you need to do: Internet Explorer is installed already (Figure 4.1). If you're using Windows 95, you may be able to install Internet Explorer from your Windows CD-ROM, but it's a very old version. (We'd recommend that Windows 98 users upgrade to the latest version too, but the version you currently have isn't as outdated so you may be happy to put this off for a while.)

> *Make sure you select Outlook Express from the list of items to install which will be displayed. We will use this program for e-mail and news (see Chapter 5).*

You can find the latest version of Internet Explorer (which is free) on the cover CD-ROM of almost any computing or Internet-related magazine. If you have Internet access already, you can download it from Microsoft's Web site at http://www.microsoft.com. Start the installation, then answer a few simple questions and the new version will automatically overwrite any older version that was previously installed on your system.

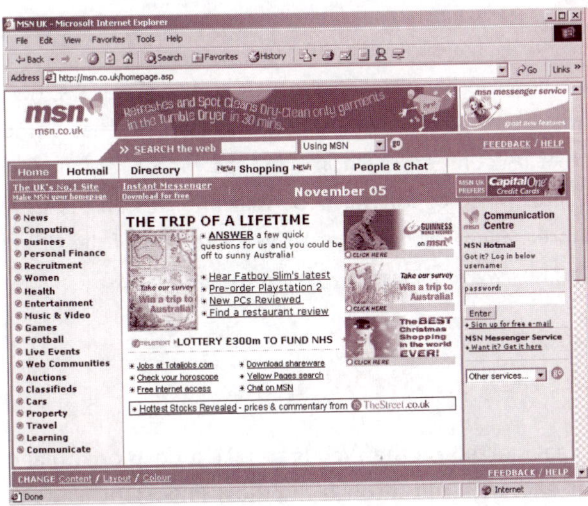

Figure 4.1

The popular Internet Explorer Web browser in action.

Installing Netscape Navigator

Although we're going to concentrate on Internet Explorer in this book, it certainly isn't the only Web browser available; it's by far the most popular, but you may still like to try something different. The best-known competitor to Internet Explorer is **Netscape** (Figure 4.2). This is unlikely to be already installed on your computer, but it's another piece of free software that you can find on magazine CD-ROMs or download from http://home.netscape.com.

> **+info**
>
> *Although you can have only one copy of Internet Explorer installed at any time (and a new copy will always replace the old copy), you can have Netscape and Opera installed alongside Internet Explorer, and you can install any number of different Netscape versions (if you really want to!).*

At the time of writing, the current version of Netscape is called **Netscape Communicator 4.7**. Along with the browser itself, it includes several other software components including an e-mail program. By the time you read this book, this version may have been replaced with the long-awaited **Netscape 6**, but this should still be free and still offer a similar set of software.

Installing Opera

A third name in the Web browser market is **Opera** (Figure 4.3). A free version, supported by advertisements, is available. It has some clever features that its competitors don't, and it's widely regarded as being a more reliable piece of software. You may find this on the CD-ROMs of some Internet magazines; alternatively, use one of the other browsers to visit http://www. operasoftware.com to find a copy.

Getting started on the Web

The best way to get started on the Web is to take a deep breath and just do it. To that end, we'll run through the most important features of Internet Explorer and then get started surfing the Web. Remember

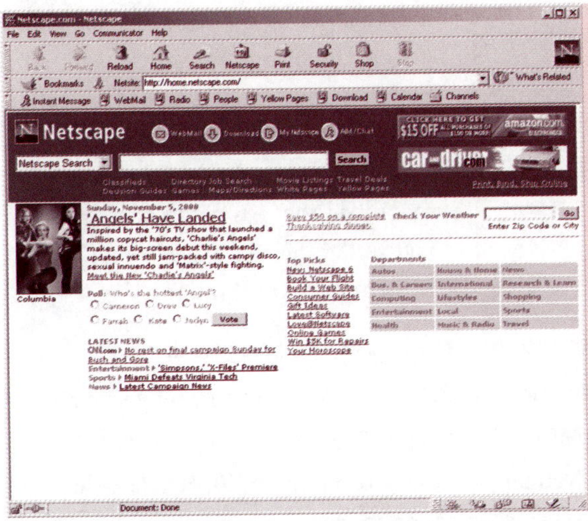

Figure 4.2

The Netscape Web browser.

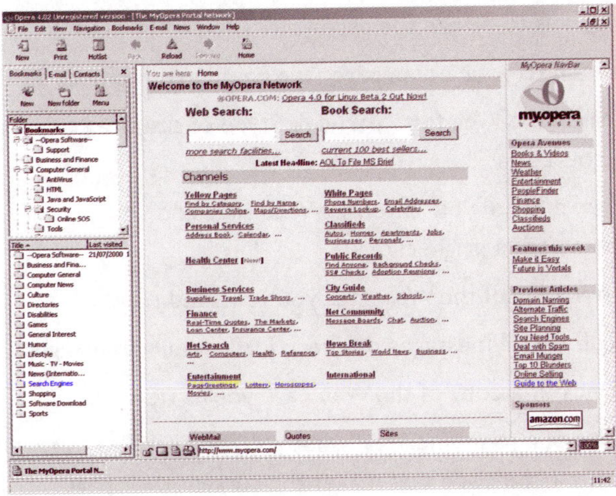

Figure 4.3

The feature-filled and increasingly popular Opera browser.

that if you make a mistake it won't have any serious consequences: you won't do your computer or the Internet any harm!

The Internet Explorer buttons

In Windows 98 and later, click on the Internet Explorer icon in the Taskbar beside the Start button (a blue 'e' icon). You can also find

+info

If you're using one of the other browsers, you'll find that the buttons and options have different names. However, most of the same options are there somewhere, and they work in a very similar way in every browser.

a similar icon on your desktop and inside the Programs folder on the Start menu in a subfolder called Internet (or Internet Tools).

Underneath the Internet Explorer menu bar there is a toolbar, shown in Figure 4.4. Here's a brief explanation of what each button does:

Back Switch to the page you visited prior to this one.

Forward After using the Back button, use this to move forward to pages you viewed recently.

Stop If a Web page is taking too long to display, click this button to stop trying to view it.

Refresh Use this to reload the page you're currently viewing.

Home Switch to your home page (see below) with one click.

Search Search the Web for a particular type of site or resource.

Favorites View a list of your favourite Web sites and visit one of them with a single click.

History View a list of the Web sites you've visited recently.

Mail Send e-mail messages or check for incoming messages.

Print Print out a copy of the Web page you're viewing.

Edit A bit of a misnomer really, but you can click this button to view the code that makes the current Web page display properly in the browser.

Figure 4.4
The Internet Explorer toolbar.

Launching Internet Explorer for the first time

Every time you launch it, Internet Explorer tries to connect to its **home page** (Microsoft Network at http://www.msn.co.uk) which isn't necessarily what you want. This is because a browser has to display a Web page when it's running, and this is the page set as the default starting page for Internet Explorer. To show this page, your browser must connect to your service provider, so there'll be a pause while your modem dials.

You can change this behaviour, of course. A popular option is to make Internet Explorer display a blank page when it starts. To do this, click on **Internet Options** in the **Tools** menu and you'll see the dialogue box shown in Figure 4.5. Click on the **Use Blank** button and confirm your choice by clicking on **OK**.

You may be happy to always start surfing from a particular Web page but would prefer it to be a *different* page. The easiest way to set your home page to something different is to visit the new site first, so let's do it that way. As an example, we'll take the Web site of the National Trust, whose URL is http://www.nationaltrust.org.uk. (Remember, a *URL* is just a fancy name for an 'address of a Web site'.)

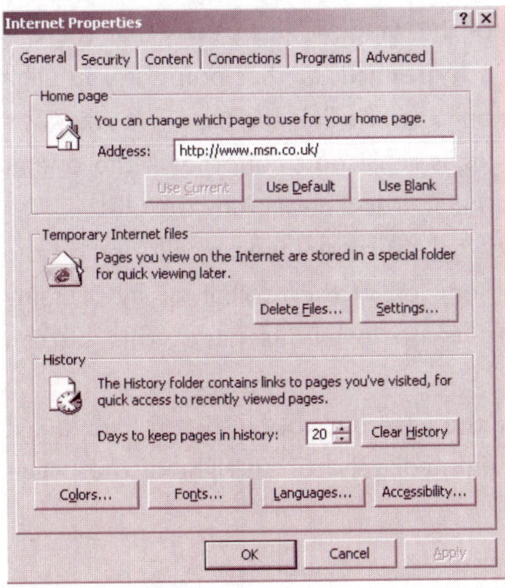

Figure 4.5

Choose your starting page by typing a URL into the box, or clicking the **Use Blank** button.

To visit this URL, click once in the text field labelled **Address** near the top of the Internet Explorer window, and type the URL. Make sure there are no typing mistakes: if there are, you might end up somewhere different, or nowhere at all! After typing the address, press **Enter** to make your browser connect to that address and display the page, and in a few moments your screen should show something similar to the screenshot in Figure 4.6. When the page appears, go back to the Internet Options dialogue we were using a minute ago and click the button marked **Use Current**. In future, Internet Explorer will connect to this site every time you launch it.

*At the moment your Internet Explorer window may be too small to see much of the Web page. You can stretch it or maximise it, of course, just like any other window, but a neat alternative is to make it **Full screen**. To do this, press **F11** or choose **Full Screen** from the View menu. To switch out of Full Screen mode, do the same again.*

Activating links

When you move your mouse pointer on the screen you will see that it changes into a hand with a raised index finger when it hovers over underlined text or some of the pictures. At the same time, a URL will appear in the status bar at the bottom of the window. This shows that there is a **hyperlink** at that point. If you click once on the link, the page you are viewing is replaced by another – the one at the address specified by the URL.

+info

*To stop a page from loading, click on the **Stop** button. The effect is immediate and this will be displayed as greyed.*

You can go back to your original site at any time by clicking on the **Back** button, the one on the very left of the toolbar, or by pressing the **Backspace** key. If there is no 'previous page', this button is greyed.

If you have stopped loading the page but you wish you hadn't, just click on the **Refresh** button (immediately to the right of the previous one) or press **F5**.

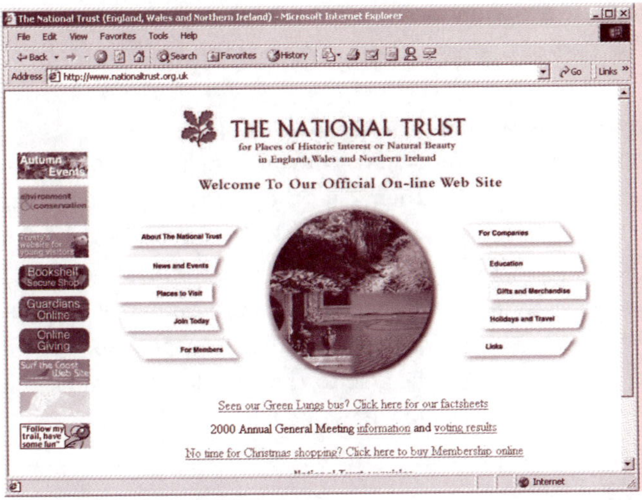

Figure 4.6

The National Trust Web site (as it appears in late 2000 – it may look a little different when you see it!).

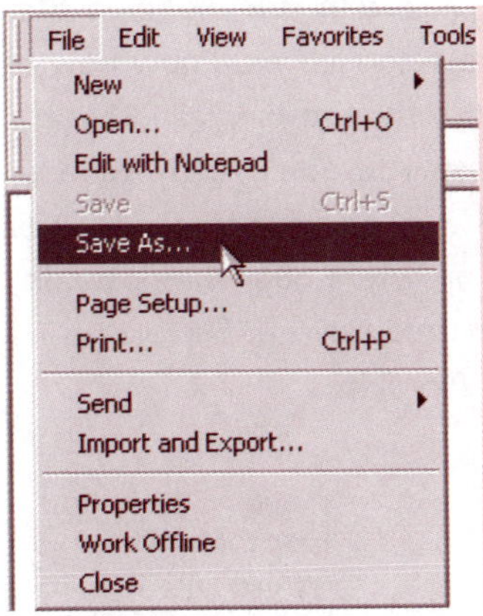

Figure 4.7

Saving a Web page to your hard disk.

Saving text and pictures

When you find an interesting page, you can save it to your hard disk. To do this, simply click on **File/Save As** (shown in Figure 4.7). In the save-file dialogue box displayed, select the folder on your hard disk where you want to save the page and choose a different name for it if you want to.

In the **Save as type** section of the dialogue you can choose whether to save the whole page (including pictures and other items) or just its text. To save the whole page, choose either the **Web**

Page, Complete option or the neater **Web Archive** option. To save just the text of the page, choose **Web Page, HTML Only** or **Text file**.

If you just want to save a picture, don't use the File/Save As option. Instead, click on the picture with your right mouse button, then, in the context menu that appears, click on **Save Picture As** (Figure 4.8). (The context menu will contain a few extra options if the picture is also a link.) As before, you will be able to choose a location and name for the saved file.

+info

To print a page, click on ***File/Print*** *or press* ***Ctrl+P****. A fairly faithful reproduction of the whole Web page will be printed on paper. The Print dialogue box gives you a few options about exactly what is printed and how.*

Saving a page address

During your Web surfing activities, you're sure to stumble upon sites that you'd like to visit again in the future. Although you know how to visit a Web page by typing its address into the browser's address bar (that wide text field labelled **Address**), you don't really want to write down and keep track of the URLs of all your favourite Web sites. Fortunately you don't have to: all browsers offer the possibility of creating what is known as a *bookmark*, and Internet Explorer is no different. It calls these stored addresses **Favorites**.

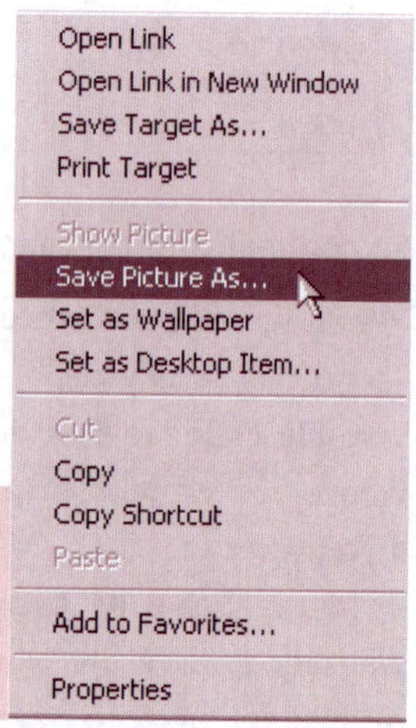

Figure 4.8

Saving a picture from a Web page.

To add the page you're viewing to your list of Favorites, open the Favorites menu and choose **Add to Favorites** (Figure 4.9). An **Add Favorite** dialogue box will appear containing a suggested name for the page (Figure 4.10). If a different name would help you remember what this item is, you can change it to anything you like. Click **OK** to confirm and a new Favorites item will be added.

There are two ways to use one of these addresses again. One is to click on **Favorites** in the Menu bar again, then on the name you chose for the Favorites item you created. The alternative is to click the **Favorites** icon on the toolbar. In this case, the browser window splits vertically into two parts and, in the left-hand window (shown in Figure 4.11) you will see your Favorites list. Click the name of the site you want to visit.

Organising your Favorites

Within a short time, your Favorites list may become too long and you'll need to do some housekeeping. To do this, you can reorganise your list by clicking on **Favorites/Organize Favorites**.

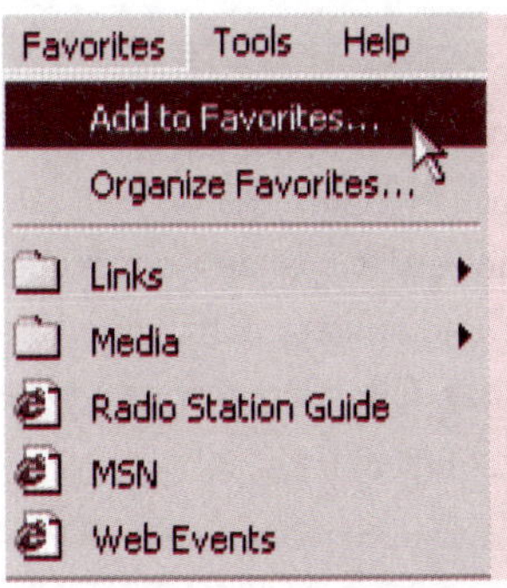

Figure 4.9

The first step in adding the page you're viewing to your list of Favorites.

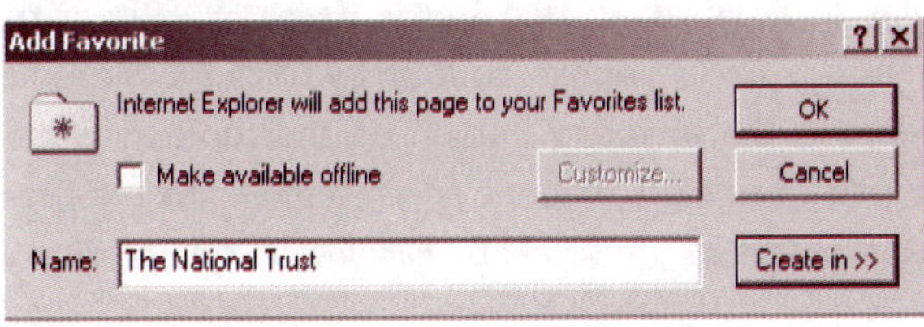

Figure 4.10

Choose a name to help you remember which site this refers to.

Figure 4.11

The Favorites window can stay open while you surf, making all your favourite sites easy to access.

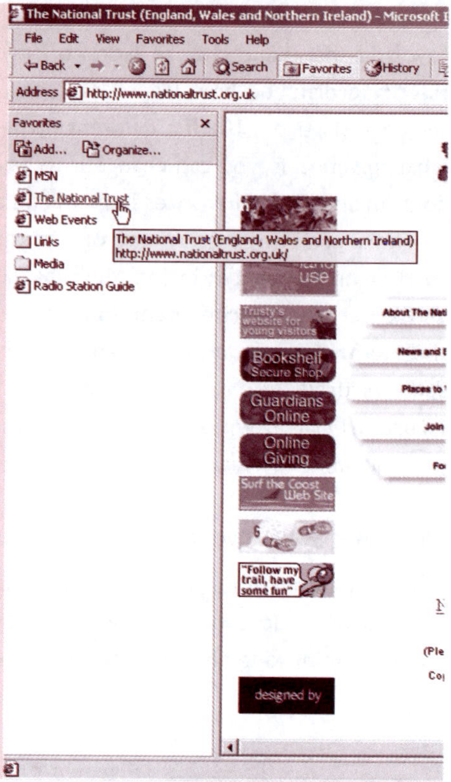

From the dialogue box that appears (shown in Figure 4.12), you can delete Favorites items, rename them, change their order, or divide them into different folders according to their subject. Changing the display order of your Favorites is very easy. Click on the one you want to move and drag it to wherever you want it.

History

Without you having to do anything, the sites you visit are automatically stored in a history folder whose contents you can explore at any time by clicking on the **History** button on the toolbar. In the left-hand window, you'll see a set of icons corresponding to the previous week and to the days of the week. By clicking on one of these,

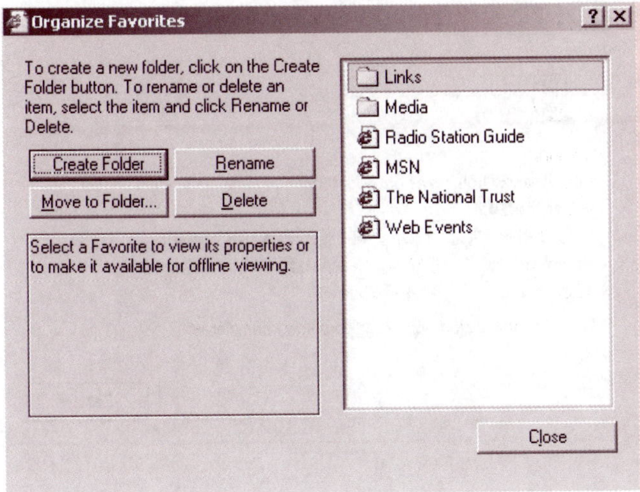

Figure 4.12

Choose Organize Favorites to reorganise your Favorites list.

you will see lists of the sites you visited on particular days. You can then visit one of these sites again simply by clicking on one of these entries.

You can modify the period your pages are kept in the history folder or clear history with the options offered in the Internet Options dialogue box that we saw earlier in this chapter.

Because you've already visited these sites, Internet Explorer may have stored copies of the pages on your hard disk. If so, you may be able to review the pages without going online. However, not all pages are stored in this way, so this isn't guaranteed.

Downloading files

Most of the links you click on a Web page will fetch a new Web page to display in the browser, but links can point to any type of file at all, including spreadsheets, databases, applications, and other types of file that you can **download** (copy to your own hard disk) for later use.

When you click on the link, a save-file dialogue will ask you to choose a folder on your hard disk and, while the transfer is happening, another dialogue box will keep you informed of the progress (Figure 4.13). If you find that it is too slow, you can cancel the download without disconnecting from your service provider by clicking on the **Cancel** button, and perhaps try downloading the same file again later.

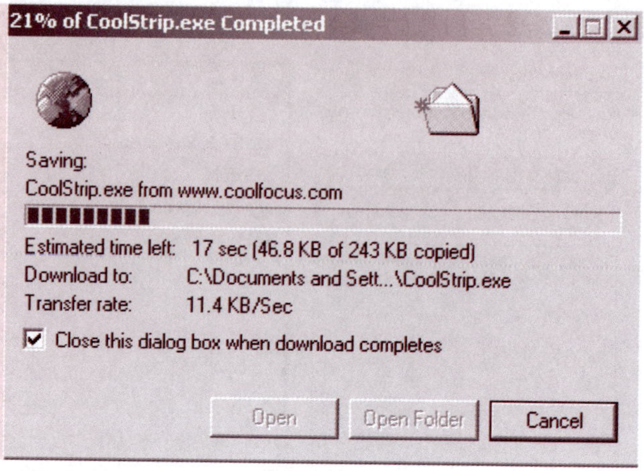

Figure 4.13

Internet Explorer keeps you posted on the progress of the file you're downloading.

During the transfer, there's nothing stopping you from carrying on exploring the Web. Windows is a multi-tasking system and Internet Explorer fully supports this mode. This will cause your download to happen a little more slowly, though, because your modem has to divide its energies between retrieving the file you are downloading *and* the new page you're trying to view.

Closing Internet Explorer

Nothing easier: as with all software running in Windows, click on **File/Close** or on the  icon in the upper-right corner of the window, or press **Alt+F4**. This doesn't interrupt the connection to your ISP, but if you don't have any other Internet-related programs open you may see a dialogue box asking if you'd like to disconnect.

5

E-mail and newsgroups

- **How e-mail works**
- **How to write messages**
- **Setting up Outlook Express**
- **The Outlook Express window**

It doesn't have quite the same appeal as the World Wide Web, but what e-mail lacks in glitz it more than makes up for in usefulness. That accounts for why e-mail has become the most widely used of all the Internet's services: a message can be typed quickly; one or more computer files can be attached as 'extras' to be sent along with it; and the whole lot can be on the computer of someone on the other side of the world in a matter of minutes. All for much less than the price of a first-class stamp!

How e-mail works

E-mail is a 'real time' system: if you send a message to a friend and you both have permanent Internet connections, your friend will receive this message almost immediately. But what happens if your friend uses an ISP for his connection? He may not be online when you send your message to him, so of course he can't receive it. In his absence, your mail must go somewhere to wait until he *is* online.

This is where e-mail servers come in. These applications run on computers permanently linked to the Internet. The protocol used for *sending* messages is known as **SMTP (Simple Mail Transfer Protocol)**. A second protocol is used for *receiving* messages, known as **POP3 (Post Office Protocol**, currently in its third version). POP works as though you had a post office box with your username on it. All the messages that arrive for you are placed inside your personal mailbox on your ISP's server, and they'll wait there until you go online and use your e-mail program to connect to the mail server and see what's waiting to be collected (if anything).

> *E-mail won't wait in this box for ever, but if you go on holiday for a few weeks and can't go online to check your e-mail while you're away, it will still be waiting when you get back. Most ISPs will delete e-mail if the mailbox hasn't been checked for several months.*

How to write messages

A message composed in e-mail is made up of two parts: the **header** and the **body** of the message.

Message header

The header is broken down into the following pieces:

To: The address to which the message is being sent. This would be something like joe.bloggs@freeserve.net, meaning that the message will be sent to the mailbox named joe.bloggs at the Freeserve ISP service.

From: The address from which the message was sent (in other words, your e-mail address).

Reply to: A reply address. Usually this is the same as the e-mail address of the sender, but it's possible to specify a different reply address if, for example, you're sending mail from your business e-mail address but you'd like replies sent to you at home.

Subject: A one-line indication of the topic of the message.

CC: Short for carbon copy. You can type extra e-mail addresses of other people who should receive a copy of the message. (You could alternatively include these extra addresses in the To field, separating each address with a semi-colon.)

BCC: Short for blind carbon copy. This works like the CC field but hides the list of other recipients from view so that the reader won't know who else received a copy.

Attachments: One or more separate computer files that are being sent with the message.

When you start to write a new e-mail message, you'll see text fields for most of these fields and you can fill in the ones you need to.

Message body

This is the main blank section of the message window where you type the message itself. E-mail is an informal method of communication: don't follow the traditions of letter-writing, but keep it short and to the point.

General rules

The relaxed style doesn't give you licence to be careless! Pay attention to your style, especially to your spelling.

NEVER TYPE A MESSAGE IN CAPITAL LETTERS! ON THE INTERNET, WHERE LIVE SPEECH HAS ONLY RECENTLY BECOME POSSIBLE, TYPING IN CAPITALS IS REGARDED AS SHOUTING AND WILL PROMPT SOME ANGRY RESPONSES FROM YOUR RECIPIENTS.

Don't include your home address, phone number, or place of work (or school) in a message unless the recipient really needs to know them (and doesn't know them already). This is partly in keeping with the *'It's not letter-writing!'* rule, and partly for basic security reasons. Make sure your children understand and observe this rule, too.

Never, ever, include your credit card details or your username and password in an e-mail message. Anyone who has a valid reason for wanting these details will also be able to offer you a secure way of transmitting them: they wouldn't dream of asking you to send them by e-mail!

Try to resist the temptation to use 'stationery' for e-mail messages (background images, patterns and pictures). They make a normal tiny e-mail message much larger (usually between 10 and 50 times as large). E-mail is supposed to be quick and simple, not a work of art. People who receive a lot of e-mail each day won't want to talk to you if all your messages take 10 times as long to download as everyone else's!

Confidentiality

Never forget that your service provider has the ability to read e-mail messages you send via their computer, as does the administrator of any other server through which the message passes on its way to the intended recipient. Of course, your message is just one of millions, but e-mail is certainly not regarded as a secure or private form of communication – far from it.

> *Because e-mail is such an immediate and relaxed form of communication, think twice and re-read what you've written before clicking the* ***Send*** *button. If you've written a rude or angry reply to a message, are you sure it's justified? More importantly, are you sure you haven't misunderstood the intention of the writer? Remember that messages you receive may sometimes seem a little brusque simply because they were written quickly.*

Returned mail

When you sign up with an ISP, you'll automatically be assigned your own mailbox and e-mail account. If you decide to cancel your subscription and switch to a different ISP, that e-mail account will also be cancelled. When someone tries to send e-mail to you at that account, the message will be *bounced back* to them (in other words, it will be returned to them with the error message 'User unknown').

If you switch to a different ISP, you will need to let all your friends, family and colleagues know your new e-mail address. This could take some time, and some may still send you messages that will never reach you. Therefore it's best to hang onto your old account for a while after signing up for your new one, just to be sure you don't miss any important messages. Another option is to sign up for an e-mail forwarding service which will provide you with a fixed e-mail address for life (such as the service provided by Bigfoot at http://uk.bigfoot.com). Tell your correspondents this permanent address, and all received messages will be automatically forwarded to your current ISP e-mail address. If that changes, just go back to the forwarding service's Web site and modify your account details so that they'll forward e-mail to the new ISP address instead.

How to save on your telephone bill

Those with a permanent connection to the Internet (or those who use it at work) can take their time and read their messages one by one, and reply to each of them carefully and at length. As this is probably not the case for you, it's useful to know how to do as much as possible before actually connecting.

The trick is to go online and retrieve any e-mail messages waiting for you but *don't start reading them yet!* Instead, disconnect from the Net first. Then you can take your time preparing replies without feeling rushed by those expensive minutes ticking by. This is known as **working offline**: most e-mail programs have a folder called an Outbox where messages you want to send are stored if you're not online. When you're ready, reconnect and send all those messages in one batch, quickly and very cheaply, with no wasted online time.

Another option is to sign up for a ***Web-based e-mail account*** *such as Hotmail* ***(http://www.hotmail.com)*** *or Yahoo! Mail* ***(http://uk.mail.yahoo.com)****. Because you access this mail account from a Web site, it's not dependent upon which ISP you use, and you can access your e-mail from any Net-connected computer in the world.*

Setting up Outlook Express

Both Internet Explorer and Netscape, the two most-used browsers, include e-mail programs, but these are by no means the only options. Two of the best-known e-mail programs are Pegasus Mail (for Windows, from http://www.pmail.com) and Eudora (for Windows and Macintosh, from http://www.eudora.com), which are comparable in their quality.

However, Microsoft offers its own e-mail program, Outlook Express, with Internet Explorer and includes it with Windows, and as a result that's become one of the most popular e-mail programs in use. Since you have Internet Explorer, you already have Outlook Express, so that's what we'll concentrate on for the remainder of this chapter.

Starting Outlook Express

The first time you open Outlook Express, you will have to specify some options so that it can connect to the e-mail and news servers of your service provider and manage your e-mail. Apart from your name and your e-mail address, you must specify the Internet addresses of these servers (which your service provider should have told you).

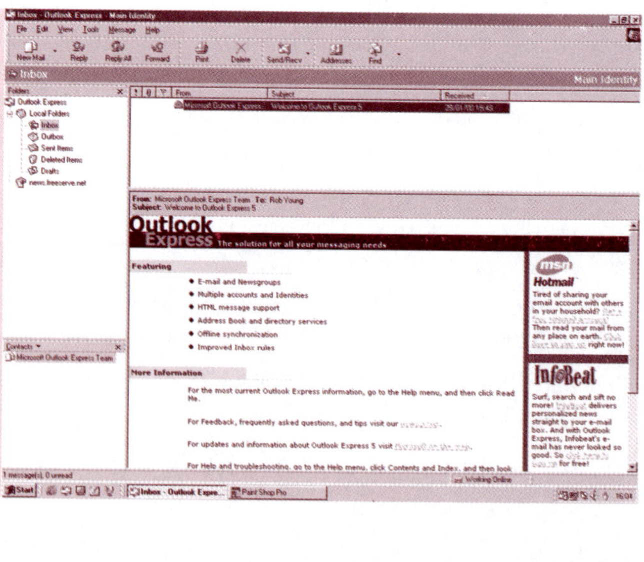

Figure 5.1

The Outlook Express window.

Adding an e-mail account

When you signed up for your ISP account, the CD-based setup almost certainly created an e-mail account for you in Outlook Express (Figure 5.1). Nevertheless, it's useful to know how to do that in case you ever want to add extra e-mail accounts.

Click on **Tools/Accounts** to display the Internet Accounts dialogue box shown in Figure 5.2. Here you should see the account created by your ISP's setup program, or one you created when prompted after starting Outlook Express for the first time. You can modify its settings (if, for example, you chose one of the wrong ones by mistake) by clicking on the **Properties** button. A dialogue box with five tabs will open, allowing you to make the necessary changes.

To create a new e-mail account, click the **Add** button, then the **Mail** option, which will start the Wizard that helps you create new accounts. In four simple steps you'll enter your name (or the name you want recipients to see when they receive mail from this account); the e-mail address of this account; the names of your ISP's e-mail servers, which your ISP will tell you; and the username and password you use to access your incoming e-mail mailbox. After completing these steps, you'll see an additional account has been added to the list in the **Internet Accounts** dialogue box.

At the moment your new account has a dull name like mail.myprovider.com. To change this to something friendlier, select the account name, click the **Properties** button, and replace that name with something better at the top of the dialogue box that appears.

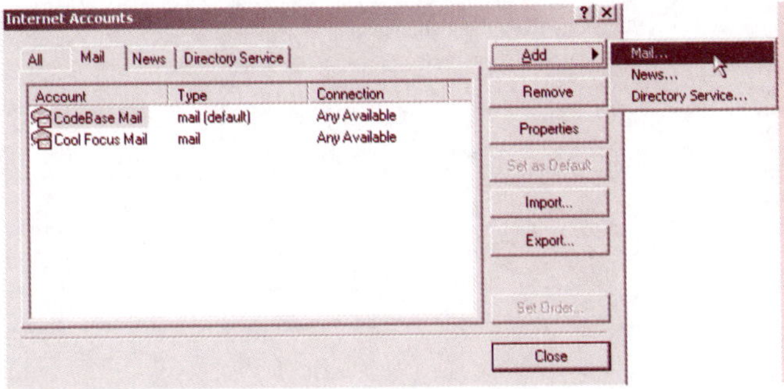

Figure 5.2

The Outlook Express dialogue box where you manage your e-mail and news accounts.

Main e-mail options

By opening the Tools menu and selecting Options, you can customise the behaviour of Outlook Express to suit yourself. Most of the options are set at sensible settings, so you shouldn't need to change much, but we'll show you the main options here and point out the ones that UK users should adjust. Because you'll also use this program for accessing newsgroups in Chapter 6, we'll adjust the settings relating to newsgroups too.

> **+info**
>
> *Your username and password for your primary (or only) e-mail account will usually be the same as those you use to dial up to the Internet and log on to your service provider.*

General tab

On this tab, remove the checkmark beside **Send and receive messages at startup** (Figure 5.3). Often you'll want to start Outlook Express to look for a message, or reply to messages, but not actually go online yet, and it would be irritating to have your computer try to dial up.

Figure 5.3

The General tab of Outlook Express's Options dialogue box.

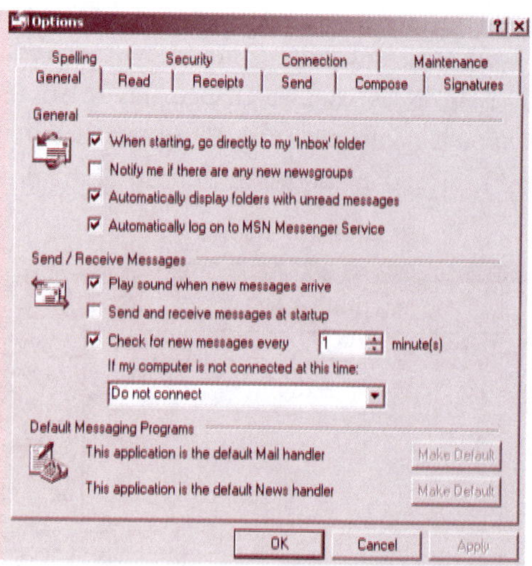

Send tab

It's a good idea to remove the checkmark beside the option **Send messages immediately**. This allows you to work offline, as mentioned earlier in the chapter, by putting your outgoing messages into the Outbox folder until you go online. Otherwise, as soon as you finish writing one message your computer goes online to send it, even though you might have five more to write!

In the Mail Sending Format section choose **Plain Text**. Your correspondents will thank you for it, since they will be able to read all of your text much better than if you had chosen HTML. The same should be selected in the News Sending Format section.

Signatures tab

A Signature is a short piece of text automatically added to each outgoing message. It contains your name, and it might also include your e-mail address, Web site URL, company details (but not usually your home address or phone number), and perhaps a short quote that sums up your outlook on life. (Weird? Yes, but it's another common 'e-mail thing'!)

Click on **New** to create a signature, and you'll see an item named **Signature #1** appear. Click on **Rename** and type a better name for it, such as **Business Signature**, or **Personal Signature**. In the text area below, type the text that should appear in the message when you include this signature (Figure 5.4). A signature should be kept fairly short: about 5 lines is the maximum, so the small size of the text box in this dialogue should be taken as a hint. Remember, it's a signature, not a CV.

Spelling tab

The option to spell-check your e-mail messages will be available only if you've installed Microsoft Office 97 or later (or a part of Office that includes a spell-checking option, such as Microsoft Word). On this tab, you can choose the default spell-checking language to use, and choose related options.

Figure 5.4

A typical example of a simple signature.

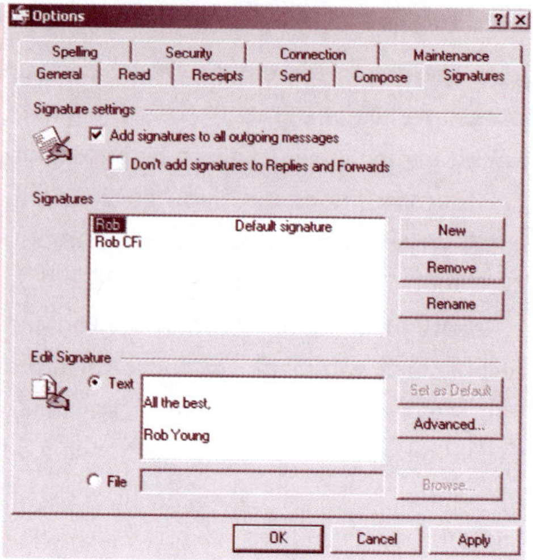

The Outlook Express window

The Outlook Express window consists of four separate sections, or 'panes'. You can stretch or shrink each section by moving the mouse over the border between two sections and dragging.

- The upper-right window displays the list of messages in the currently selected folder. For example, if the Inbox folder is selected, you'll see the list of messages in the Inbox. Messages are shown here as just their header (the To, From, Subject and Date fields).
- The lower-right section is the optional Preview pane: when you click on one of the message headers in the pane above, the body of that message will be shown here.
- The lower-left section is your Contacts list, showing all the people whose addresses you've added to your Address Book (more about that later in the chapter). To send a new message to one of these people, double-click the name.
- The upper-left window is the folders list. At start-up it contains five folders (described below), but you can add as many folders as you like and drag messages from the message list on the right into any folder to organise your messages in any way that makes sense to you.

The first time you start Outlook Express, the folder list contains these five folders:

Inbox. When new e-mail messages arrive, this is where they will be placed.

Outbox. This will contain messages that you've written but haven't sent yet. Once you click on **Send/Receive**, these will be sent and automatically moved into the Sent Items folder.

Sent Items. This folder holds items that have been successfully sent. This is your confirmation that a message really has been sent.

Deleted Items. Sometimes it's necessary to tidy your e-mail folders and get rid of unwanted mail. When you delete a message, this is where it goes (much like Windows' own Recycle Bin).

Drafts. If you've written a message that you don't want to send straight away (perhaps you haven't finished it), instead of clicking **Send**, choose Save from the File menu, or press **Ctrl+S**. The message will be stored in the Drafts folder. When you want to finish the message, open Drafts and double-click the message header. When you click the **Send** button, the message will be removed from Drafts and placed in the Outbox.

If you go to View/Layout, you can check and uncheck boxes to hide or display various panes in Outlook Express. For example, you can hide the Preview pane, or choose where it should be. (With the Preview pane hidden, you'll have to double-click a message header to read it.)

Sending an e-mail message

Click on the **New Message** button, or on File/New/Mail Message, or press **Ctrl-N**. A new message window will open (as shown in Figure 5.5). You'll see the fields we mentioned earlier in the chapter, and the ones you need to complete are the **To** field, where you enter the e-mail address of the recipient, and the **Subject** field (giving a brief description of the topic).

*To move from one field to another, press the **Tab** key. To go through the boxes in reverse order, hold down the **Shift** key while pressing the **Tab** key.*

Figure 5.5

An e-mail message ready to be sent.

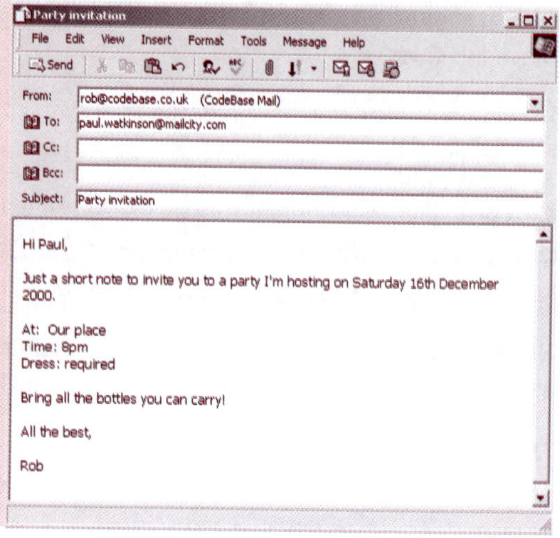

Depending upon your Signature settings, covered earlier, you may see your default signature in the main part of the window already. If your signature hasn't been added automatically, you can open the Insert menu, move down to Signature, and select which signature you'd like to use. Then, of course, you write the body of the message.

Never attach large files unless the recipient is expecting you to send them. Anything over 100Kb qualifies as 'large', and Outlook Express shows the size of a file in the Attach field to help you avoid mistakes.

If you wish, you can send copies of any computer files with this message as **attachments** – perhaps a picture, a program, a sound file, anything. To do this, click the paperclip button on the toolbar and you'll be able to choose the file from a standard open-file dialogue box. (You can also drag-and-drop a file's icon into this window to attach that file.) The attached file is shown as an icon in the **Attach** field (this field isn't visible unless one or more files have been attached).

+info

Outlook Express displays a number in blue beside folders sometimes. This indicates how many unread messages that folder contains. To find out how many messages are in a particular folder in total, click that folder to open it, then look at Outlook Express's status bar.

Finally, click the **Send** button on the toolbar of the message window. The window will close and the message will be added to the Outbox. If you open the Outbox folder, you'll see the header of the message.

Sending and receiving messages

The only way to find out whether there's any mail waiting to be received is by connecting to your ISP and clicking the **Send/Receive** button on the toolbar. When you do this, any messages waiting in your Outbox will be sent and you'll see a dialogue box showing you the progress of messages being sent and then messages being received (if any).

If you look in your Sent Items folder, you should see that all the messages that were waiting in the Outbox are here instead.

Select the Inbox folder, and you'll see the incoming messages arriving in that folder. You'll also see the number beside the word **Inbox** change to indicate how many unread messages that folder now contains. Click the header of any message in the Inbox to read it in the preview pane below.

If you see a paperclip at the right-hand end of the preview window's grey bar, the message you're reading has one or more files attached (Figure 5.6). Click the paperclip to see a list of the files attached and their sizes.

If you click on one of the files, Outlook Express will ask you whether you want to open it or save it to disk. If the attachment is a picture file (identified by .jpeg or .gif extensions) you can safely open it; for other formats, it's best to save it to disk and check it for viruses before opening (see Chapter 1).

Figure 5.6

The paperclip icon indicates that there's a file attached to the message you're reading.

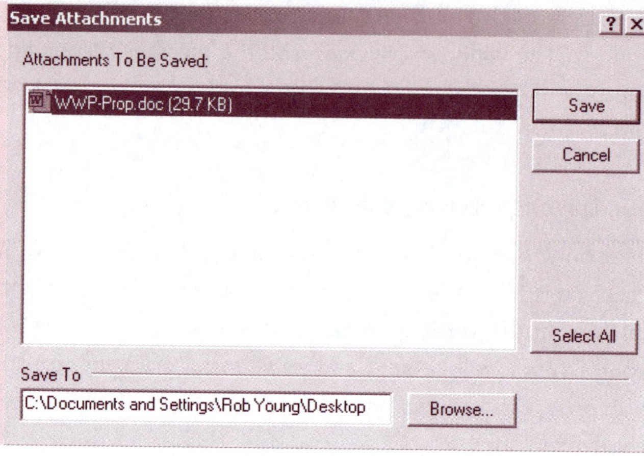

Figure 5.7

Choose **Save Attachments** if you want to choose which to save and where.

Alternatively, click on the Save Attachments option. This will let you select one or more of the attached files (Figure 5.7) and choose a folder where they should be saved.

Replying to a message

After you've read a message, you're likely to want to send a reply. Click on the **Reply** button on the toolbar. (The **Reply All** button is used only when you wish to reply to many people; for example, when you're replying to a message that was sent to a group of people and you want each to have a copy of your reply.) A window for composing a message (see Figure 5.5) will appear with the headings and the original message text. Note that the letters 'Re:' are added in front of the subject, indicating to the recipient (and yourself) that this is a response to an earlier message.

The more text there is in a message, the longer that message takes to send, so trim down any quoted text to the bare memory-jogging essentials. If anything starts with '>>' it's from an old message being quoted a second time, so it can definitely be removed!

You'll also notice that the original message is *quoted* in the reply, with a '>' sign inserted before each line. This is a courtesy to help the recipient remember what you're actually replying to, but it shouldn't be necessary to leave the whole message (and you may feel that none of it is needed).

Once you've completed your reply, click the **Send** button in the usual way to place this message in the Outbox ready for sending.

Forwarding a message

You can forward a message to another address by clicking the **Forward** button on the toolbar. The message you wish to forward will appear in the message window, and you only have to enter the address it should be forwarded to. There's nothing to stop you from adding to the text or deleting some of it. If it had an attachment, you can remove this.

Returned messages

If you get the address of the message recipient wrong, the message will be sent back to you along with a brief explanation of the reason. That explanation may not always make sense, but it usually means that there's something wrong with the address you sent the message to.

The first thing to do is to check that the address you used is correct: no spelling mistakes, and no spaces. If you're sure the address is correct, there may be a problem with the recipient's mail server, so try to send the message later in the day. If the address was wrong, create a new message (putting in the correct address this time), then copy-and-paste the body of the old message into the new one to save retyping it, and click **Send**.

Your address book

You will almost certainly end up exchanging messages with regular correspondents. In this case, instead of worrying about typing in their e-mail address every time, put them in your address book. It's a useful shortcut for several reasons: first, you don't have to remember anyone's e-mail address (or risk mistyping it!); second, you can refer to people by their real name or an alias; third, you don't have to type anything at all; fourth, you can store extra information such as phone numbers, addresses and Web site URLs in the address book, making it a complete contacts management system.

When an address is added to the address book, the person's name is included. You can also include an easy-to-type nickname; for example, in Figure 5.8, you can see we've assigned the nickname **jb** to our fictitious friend Joe Bloggs. With this contact in the address book, we can send a message to Joe in several ways:

- If the Contacts pane of Outlook Express is visible, just double-click the name **Joe Bloggs**.
- Click the **New Message** button and begin typing **Joe Bloggs** in the **To** field. Before you get far, Outlook Express should recognise this as a name from the address book and complete it for you automatically.
- Type the nickname, **jb**, into the **To** field.

If someone sends you a message, you can add them to your address book very easily. Just right-click the message header in the Inbox and choose ***Add Sender to Address Book****. To add extra details to someone's address book entry (or change existing details), click the* ***Address Book*** *icon on the toolbar, select the required contact and choose* ***Properties****.*

Figure 5.8

The address book can store vast amounts of information about each contact.

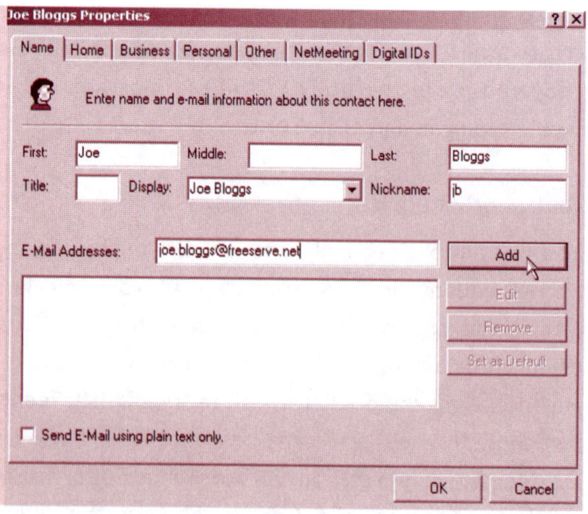

Deleting unwanted messages

After a number of weeks or months of using e-mail, your message folders will probably contain a lot of useless and out-of-date information. As a security device, deleting messages is doubly useful. To delete a message, right-click on its header and choose **Delete**, or just select the header and press the **Delete** key. The message is placed in the **Deleted Items** folder, where it will stay until you empty that folder (so you can still open the message if you need to).

Every so often you should empty the Deleted Items folder to recover the space it's using. Right-click on the folder and choose **Empty 'Deleted Items' Folder**.

Sorting your mail

Your original folders will soon fill up and you will have difficulty trying to find your files. To get some order, you need to create your own personalised folders (People, Cooking, Business, Friends, and so on) in which you can store your messages once you've read and replied to them.

To create a folder, click **File/Folder/New**. In the Create Folder dialogue box (shown in Figure 5.9), enter the name of the new folder in the **Folder name** field, select where to place the folder (usually **Local Folders** unless you'd like the new folder to be inside one of the existing folders), then click **OK**.

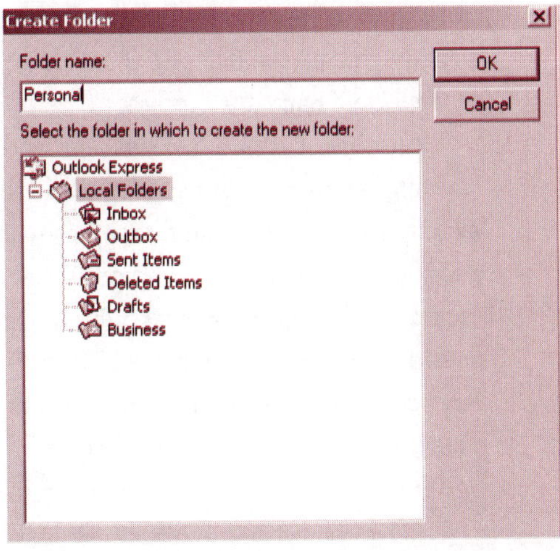

Figure 5.9

Creating additional folders to organise your e-mail messages.

6

Get the latest news!

- Newsgroups
- Using the Outlook Express newsreader
- News on the Web

Newsgroups

In the context of the Internet, 'news' doesn't mean the latest headlines from ITN. Newsgroups are more formally known as **Usenet news forums**. Usenet is like a huge notice board divided into lots of different subject-specific areas where anyone can display their questions and offer replies to questions already there (or just put their point of view on a particular topic).

> **+info** *There's one other small difference between newsgroup messages and e-mail messages: whereas e-mail messages usually arrive at their destination within seconds or minutes, newsgroup messages may not filter out to the whole Usenet network for 24 hours. The servers that make up this network aren't in constant contact, they usually connect daily to exchange new messages with each other.*

All this is done by writing and sending plain-text messages almost exactly like e-mail. In fact, many e-mail programs work with newsgroups too, including Outlook Express which we used in the previous chapter. The difference is that here you're writing text that may be read by thousands of people, so it's far more important to observe the 'rules'. So important, in fact, that the rules even have their own name: they're referred to as *netiquette* (derived, of course, from Net etiquette).

What are newsgroups?

Usenet consists of over 50,000 different newsgroups (and growing), covering thousands of different subjects. These groups work rather like 50,000 different e-mail mailboxes, all accessible to the public. Anyone can send a message to any of these groups, and anyone can read the messages received by a group. The messages themselves are just like e-mail messages with one exception: instead of sending them to an e-mail address they're sent to a newsgroup address.

Although there are tens of thousands of newsgroups available, you may not necessarily have access to all of them. Newsgroups need vast amounts of disk space: imagine the space needed to store 50,000 groups, each containing 2000 messages, for instance! So your ISP might decide to skip certain less popular groups, and many ISPs refuse to take groups that may offend their users. However, you may still be able to access missing groups through a public news server, as we'll see later in this chapter.

Netiquette

Before you get involved in the groups themselves, it pays to know the 'rules' of Usenet.

Except for in the 'biz' (business) hierarchy of groups, and the 'announce' groups, advertising or sending commercial messages is frowned upon.

If you have a question or comment, make sure it's relevant to the group(s) you're sending it to. You'll probably never have a valid reason to send the same message to more than about five groups; usually you send messages to one group only.

There are specialist 'test' groups such as alt.test, alt.binaries.test and comp.test which you can use to get acquainted with sending messages or finding your way around your newsreader program.

Never send test messages to newsgroups that don't have the word 'test' in their names.

AS WITH E-MAIL, DON'T SHOUT! TYPING IN CAPITALS IS REGARDED AS SHOUTING, AND IT'S ONE OF THE WORST OFFENCES POSSIBLE.

Don't send file attachments to newsgroups that don't have the word 'binaries' in their names. This word is a cue that attached files are allowed, and also acts as a warning that messages in that group might be much larger than normal as a result. Users don't want to find huge messages in non-binaries groups.

When you reply to a message in a group, the program you use will *quote* the original message, just as when you reply to e-mail. However, in newsgroups it's far more important to remove anything unnecessary: there are so many messages that it's a courtesy to other users to keep each as short as possible. In fact, since the message you're replying to will still be included in the group, you don't really need to quote *any* of it.

By the same token, keep your signature as short as possible. You'll get some rude comments if you start sending two-line messages that have a 10-line signature!

Newsgroup lingo

Newsgroups have also evolved their own peculiar set of terms and definitions. First, although the whole thing takes place using a form of e-mail, a message to a newsgroup is referred to as an **article**. And you don't *send* an article, you *post* it (so you may see articles termed *postings* as well). Here are a few more oddities:

Spam Spam is an article sent to multiple newsgroups without any thought to whether it's relevant. Most spam is an attempt at cheap advertising (which has a success rate of roughly 0% in newsgroups, but a few people still try it). The word comes from an old Monty Python sketch (ask in the **alt.fan.monty-python** group for a copy!).

Flame A 'flame' is a rude response to an article. You're likely to get flamed if you don't follow the netiquette of newsgroups. In some cases, newsgroups can get so carried away with their internal arguments that the entire group descends into 'flame warfare', with little of interest being said.

FAQ This stands for Frequently Asked Questions, and it's a list of questions with answers. Many newsgroups publish an FAQ regularly, explaining the basics of the topic they're covering so that they can avoid wasting time and effort answering the same simple questions repeatedly. (You'll find FAQs on many Web sites and elsewhere on the Internet – it's become a widespread term.)

Smileys

In spoken English, the speaker's intonation helps to convey the true meaning of what he's saying. For example, you can usually recognise sarcastic humour by the tone of voice or physical gestures, although the words may say something different. In e-mail messages and newsgroup articles you don't have these aids to understanding, so they have been replaced with little symbols designed out of keyboard characters.

These little symbols are called 'emoticons' or 'smileys', and you read them by tilting your head to the left. So when you see this message:

I've just heard that Bill's back :-(

you can tell that the writer regards this as sad news. But if the message read:

I've just heard that Bill's back :-)

it's clear that the writer is pleased about it. You can find lots more smileys at http://www.cynet.net/smile.html and http://www.pop.at/smileys.

Cross posting

Cross posting means sending the same message to more than one group. As mentioned earlier, you should always keep the number of groups to a bare minimum and be absolutely sure that your message is relevant to the groups you send it to. You can send a message to multiple groups by including each newsgroup name in the **Newsgroups** field of the message, with each separated by a comma or semi-colon.

Public servers

Some service providers do not want to offer newsgroups at all; others offer only a limited number of groups. This leaves you with two problems: how can you tell whether a particular group exists at all, and if it does, where can you access it?

There are two useful Web sites that can help. The first is http://www.magma.ca/~leisen/mlnh. This is a 'master list' of newsgroups that will help you determine whether there's a group dedicated to your favourite subject, and what it's called.

If your ISP doesn't provide the group you want through its own news server, you need a *public access* news server. For a list of public access servers, go to http://www.newzbot.com (Figure 6.1). You could also visit http://www. deja.com, covered later in this chapter.

Using the Outlook Express newsreader

As with e-mail in Chapter 5, we're going to use Microsoft's Outlook Express for our examples: after all, you have a copy already, you know how it works, and you've done most of the setting up. However, there are other newsreader programs you can use instead if you'd like to

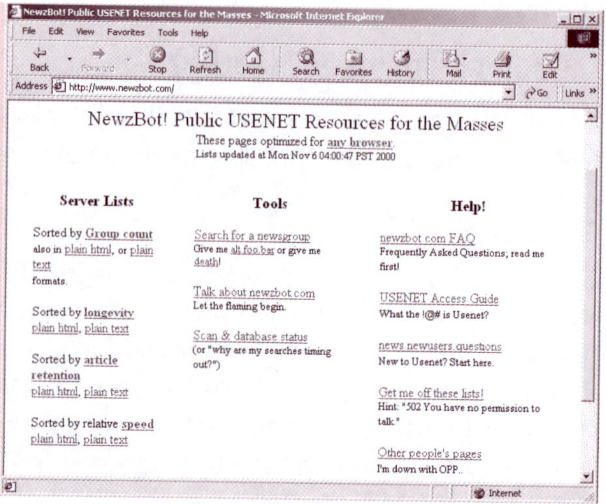

Figure 6.1

Newzbot can help you access a newsgroup that your ISP doesn't provide.

give them a try. Two of the best known are Agent and its free counterpart Free Agent, both from http://www.forteinc.com. Another popular free newsreader is the oddly named TIFNY from http://www.tifny.com.

Creating a news account

To work with newsgroups in Outlook Express, go to its **Tools** menu and choose **Newsgroups** (or press **Ctrl+W**).

If you haven't already set up a news account in Outlook Express, the Wizard dialogue box will appear to help you create one step by step. You'll be prompted to enter some straightforward information such as your name and e-mail address. You'll also need to know the name of your ISP's news server: this will usually be news.serviceprovider.co.uk, but your ISP can tell you if you're not sure.

At any time, you can create another news account just as easily. Go to Tools/Accounts, click the **Add** button and click **News** to start this Wizard again. You can also modify an existing account by choosing the News tab, selecting your news account and clicking the **Properties** button.

Your news server for the new account will appear at the bottom of Outlook Express's folder list, so you can also switch to newsgroups by simply clicking this item.

The first connection

The first time you use a news account you've created, a message will appear prompting you to download a list of newsgroups available on this news server. Accept by clicking the **Yes** button and then wait while the list of groups is fetched. A dialogue box will appear for you to monitor the downloading (Figure 6.2). This can sometimes take five minutes or so, depending on the total number of groups available on the server, but it only has to happen once: the list will be stored on your computer for future use.

Figure 6.2

The first time you connect to a news server, Outlook Express will download a list of available newsgroups.

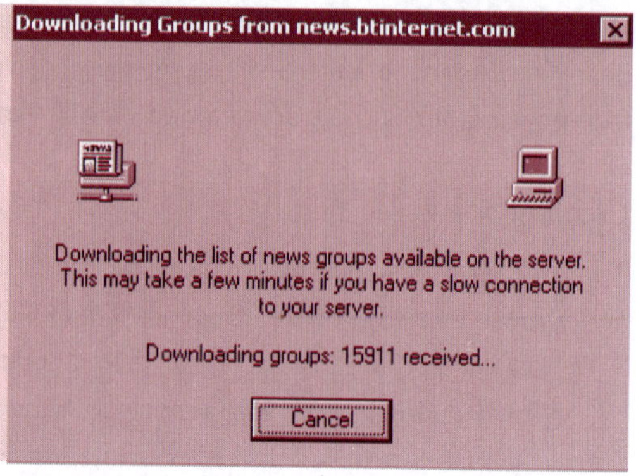

Figure 6.3

Browse through the groups alphabetically, or type a keyword to find matching group names.

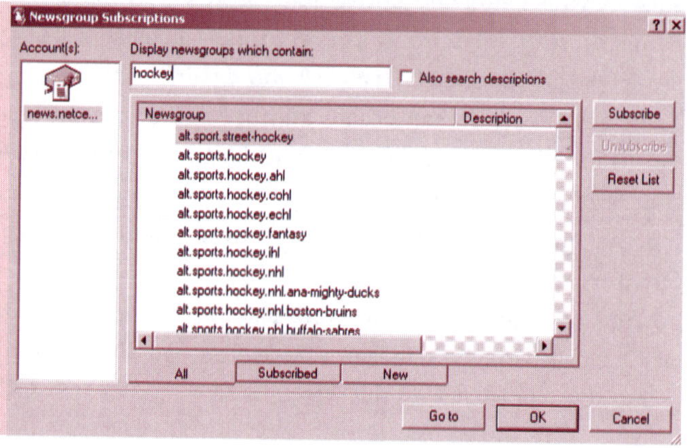

Subscribing to newsgroups

Next, you need to *subscribe* to one or more groups. The effect of this operation is to display their names in the folder list so that you can easily retrieve the articles that they contain. Click the Newsgroups button on Outlook Express's toolbar (or choose Tools/Newsgroups) to display the Newsgroup Subscriptions window shown in Figure 6.3.

This window contains an alphabetical list of all the groups available on the news server. You can see that this tabbed page is labelled **All**. If you subscribe to one or more groups you can click the **Subscribed** tab to see a list of only the groups you're currently subscribed to.

Working through tens of thousands of groups alphabetically isn't very user-friendly: a better option is to type a keyword into the field at the top. Only group names containing this word will be displayed.

To view a newsgroup without subscribing to it, select it and click the **Go To** button. To subscribe to a group, click the **Subscribe** button. You can select any number of groups to subscribe to in the same way (although we recommend you start with just one or two) and click **OK** when you're done. You'll see your subscribed groups in the folder list.

If you chose **Go To**, you'll also see the group name in the folder list. You can subscribe to it by right-clicking it and choosing **Subscribe**.

Cancelling a subscription

Click on Tools/Newsgroups, select the group that you want to cancel your subscription for and click on **Unsubscribe**. Click **OK** when you're done. You can also unsubscribe from a group by right-clicking its name in the folder list and choosing **Unsubscribe**.

Reading the headers of a group

Unlike e-mail, initially only the **headers** of news messages are downloaded. If someone sends you an e-mail message, you'll usually want to read it, so it has to be downloaded, but you won't necessarily be interested in every single article in a newsgroup.

To fetch the headers of a group, you need to be connected to the corresponding news server. By clicking on the small + at the left of the name of the server in Outlook Express's folder list, the list of groups you've subscribed to is displayed.

Click once on the name of the group that you want to read and the transfer of the headers will begin. Only the headers posted after your last transfer will be transferred, up to a maximum of 300.

+info

*The maximum number of 300 headers is because some groups are incredibly popular and generally receive thousands of messages each day. Setting a maximum ensures that you don't have to wait for hours for the latest messages to arrive. You can click the **Get Next Headers** button on the toolbar to get another 300, or change the maximum amount by going to Tools/Options/Read.*

Articles are sorted into **threads**. A thread is a set of articles which all have the same subject line and are part of an ongoing conversation. The first article in a thread will have a little + sign by its name: click that to reveal all the replies (and replies to replies, and so on) that relate to that first article.

Reading an article

To read the content of an article, you just need to click once on its header. The text of the article is then downloaded from the server (along with any attached files) and displayed in the Preview pane, in the same way as with e-mail.

Although you *can* simply work your way through the articles downloading and reading the ones you're interested in, you might prefer to work with newsgroup articles offline instead, as you do with e-mail. We'll look at how to do this in the section entitled *Reading the news offline*.

Replying to an article

With the news, you have two choices: either reply to the group (where everyone will be able to read the reply), or reply to the author directly by e-mail (the author will be the only one to read it). In general, unless the reply would involve some very personal or irrelevant details, it's best to reply to the group. This way, any other readers can benefit from your reply too.

> *Unless you're replying only by e-mail, don't forget to remove most (or all!) of the original message from your reply before sending it.*

With the message displayed (either in the Preview pane or in a separate message window), click either one of the two **Reply** buttons on the toolbar depending on which type of reply you want to send. You can also choose **Reply All** from the Message menu which sends an e-mailed reply to the author as well as posting the reply to the group.

After you've composed your reply, click on the **Send** button in the left-hand corner of the window.

Posting a new article

When you send a reply to an existing article, you are continuing the thread. But if you have a completely new question to ask, or observation to make, you want to create a brand new article and (hopefully) start a new thread. To do this, click the **New Message** button on Outlook Express's toolbar.

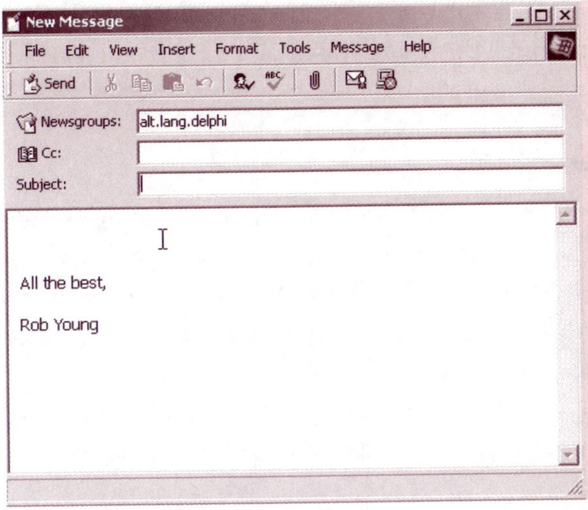

Figure 6.4

The target newsgroup is shown in the top field, but you can click the **Newsgroups** button to select others.

In the **Newsgroups** field at the top of the message window you'll see the name of the currently selected newsgroup (Figure 6.4). If this is the name of the group you want to send the message to, you can carry on. If it isn't, click the word **Newsgroups** to its left to select the required groups.

Next, type a subject for the message. Avoid using meaningless subjects like 'Help!' or 'Please read this' – people are unlikely to download your article if they can't tell what it's about! Finally, of course, write the message itself and click the **Send** button.

Attaching a file

You can easily attach a file to a newsgroup message just as you do with e-mail messages: by clicking the paperclip icon on the toolbar of the message window and selecting the required file.

Remember to do this only when the word **binaries** appears in the name of the group. In some cases there are several groups for a particular topic, one of which allows binaries and the rest of which don't. As an example, a graphics application called Lightwave has two newsgroups: comp.graphics.apps.lightwave and alt.binaries.3d.lightwave. If you have a relevant file to contribute, send it to the second of those.

However, it's reasonable to send a message without the attachment to the first group to tell them that you've sent a file to the binaries group that they may find useful.

Reading the news offline

When you download the headers of a group, it's tempting to look down the list of subjects and click on anything interesting to read it straight away. It's similar to surfing the Web, and you can work this way if you want to. A cheaper way, though, is to work offline as much as possible, just as you do with e-mail.

Select each of your subscribed newsgroups in turn to download the latest batches of headers, then disconnect from the Internet and follow these steps:

1. Go to the File menu and click **Work Offline**.
2. Select a group from the folder list on the left to view the headers you downloaded for it.
3. If any subject line seems interesting, right-click it and choose **Download Message Later** (or, if the message is part of an interesting thread, **Download Conversation Later**).
4. A downward arrow will now appear to the left of the header.
5. Repeat the steps above for all messages and all groups until you've marked all the messages and threads that seem worth reading.
6. Open the Tools menu and choose **Synchronize All**. If you're prompted to Connect, say 'yes' to the prompt. Outlook Express will connect to your news server to download all the messages you have marked (including their attachments, if they have any).
7. Disconnect from the Internet again and you can read the messages you've downloaded at your leisure.

News on the Web

Deja.com is a Web site from which you can search Usenet for either a newsgroup or (even more usefully) text in a news article. In fact, you can even browse through the articles in any newsgroup using your browser instead of your newsreader.

The Deja.com site has grown to offer a lot more than newsgroup searching, but that's what made it famous, and you can reach that section of its site with the URL http://www.deja.com/usenet (Figure 6.5). Once you're there, you can pick a news hierarchy from the front page to browse through, look for a newsgroup covering a particular subject by entering a keyword into the text field at the bottom of the window, or look for articles covering the topic you're interested in by using the fields at the top of the page.

> *If you can't remember which messages you downloaded and which you didn't, go to View/Current View and click* ***Show Downloaded Messages****. This hides the headers of any messages not downloaded. When you've read the messages, go back and choose the* ***Show All Messages*** *option.*

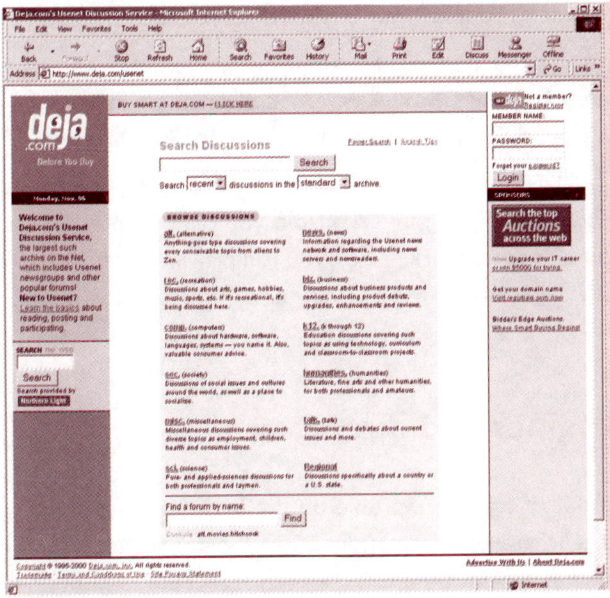

Figure 6.5

Deja.com makes it easy to find a particular newsgroup or search articles for information.

7

Searching, chatting and gaming

- **Search engines and directories**
- **Chatting on the Internet**
- **Network games**

In this chapter we gather together three extra resources you'll find useful (or at least want to try!).

- **Search engines** The quick way to find what you're looking for on the Web.
- **IRC (Internet Relay Chat)** A type of conversation channel where you can hold 'conversations' with one or more people, talking by typing messages back and forth in real time.
- **Network games** With a games console, you can only play against the computer. With network games, you can play against other people, each one sitting at their computer anywhere in the world.

Search engines and directories

With the amount of content available on the Internet, it's absolutely guaranteed that whatever information you're looking for, it exists on the Net somewhere. The thing that isn't guaranteed, of course, is that you'll ever find it! There's no central index of Web sites or their content as there is in a library. Fortunately, though, there are many individual Web sites that do their best to catalogue the contents of the Web, and you can use these sites to search for whatever you need. Although many of these indexing sites work in different ways and give different results, they're known by the general term **search engines** (see Figure 7.1 for an example).

What is a search engine?

A search engine is a fairly ordinary-looking Web page containing a text box (there may be a lot more on the page, but it's the text box that matters!). In that text box you type one or more words relating to the subject you're interested in, and then press **Enter**. The words you entered are sent to the server which searches through its database of catalogued sites for anything that matches. After a few seconds, it will send back a list of URLs that may (or may not) be relevant.

The list of search results varies from one search engine to another: since each uses its own methods to create its catalogue, you'll get a different list back from each search engine you visit. But although the Web sites found by the search differ, the way they're

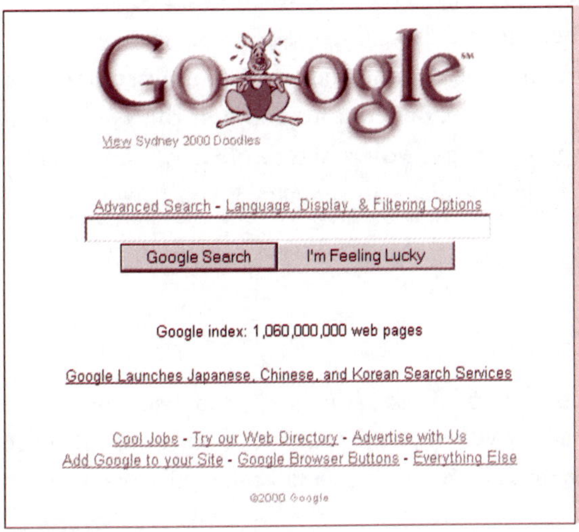

Figure 7.1

Probably the least-cluttered search engine page in existence: **www.google.com**.

presented is universal: there will be a link you can click to visit any promising-sounding Web site and a brief description (or, perhaps, a few lines quoted from the page).

In many cases a search will result in a list containing tens of thousands of Web page URLs (sometimes even hundreds of thousands). Fortunately, only the 10 most relevant pages will be listed, and you'll see buttons or links near the bottom of the page that will take you to the next 10 in the list.

Most search engines look for pages containing the word or phrase you typed into the text box. They will usually ensure that pages using the word most often appear at the top of the search-results list, but you can't be sure that one of these pages contains any useful information on the subject without visiting it.

Hit or miss?

As the whole point of searching the Internet is to find what you're looking for as quickly as possible, it's important to phrase your search clearly. For example, if you search for **racing** your search results are likely to number over a quarter of a million Web pages! Most of those pages will be irrelevant, and you may have to look a long way down the list to find pages about the type of racing you wanted. A search for **motor racing** will give far fewer results to trawl through, because links to all those pages about yacht racing, horse racing, greyhound racing (and so on) will now be gone.

There are enough useful tips and options you can use when searching for information on the Internet to fill an entire book. So what follows is just a brief introduction to some of the Web's most popular search engines to get you started. Most of the popular search sites have a Help link that you can click if you have problems using them.

AltaVista

http://uk.altavista.com

This is one of the best-known search engines, and also one of the most flexible (Figure 7.2). When you first arrive at AltaVista you'll see a row of five yellow 'tabs', with the Search tab selected. Here you can search the whole of the World Wide Web or just search for pages from UK sites, and you can search for pages in a particular language. By clicking one of the last three tabs you can search for multimedia files: pictures, video files and sounds.

Yahoo!

http://www.yahoo.co.uk

Yahoo! is probably the best-known search site in the world, but it's a little different from AltaVista and many other search engines. Although it has the usual text box allowing you to type keywords to search for, you'll also see a number of hypertext 'categories' on its front page such as Arts & Humanities, Entertainment, and Science (Figure 7.3). Instead of running a keyword search, you can just click one of these categories. A new list of sub-categories will appear, and you can burrow your way down through ever more specific category names until you find the type of site you're looking for.

If you prefer to use a keyword search, Yahoo! will present its results as two separate lists: the upper list on the page (in bold text) contains links to some of Yahoo!'s own categories which may be relevant; the lower list (in plain text) contains direct links to the Web pages found in the search.

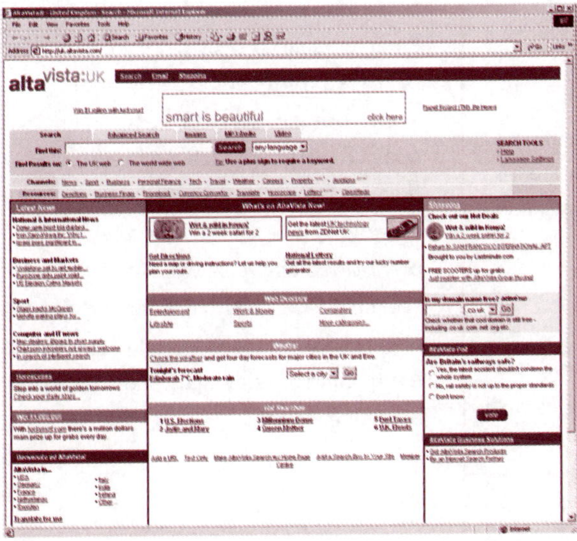

Figure 7.2

The AltaVista search engine.

Figure 7.3

Yahoo!, the workhorse of the Web.

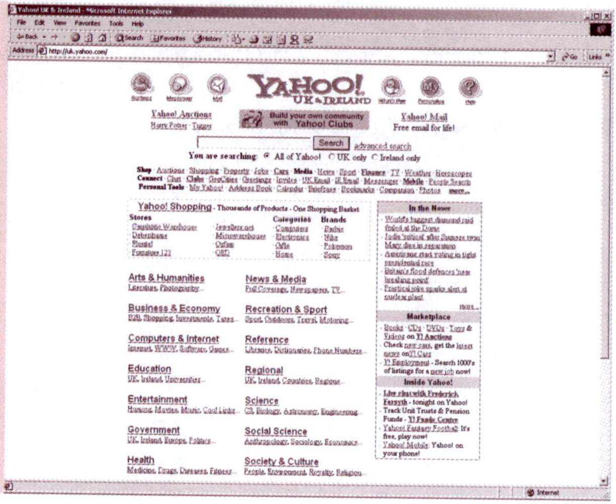

MetaCrawler

http://www.metacrawler.com

Because every search engine uses its own methods to build its indexes, each will obviously provide a different set of results in response to a search. If you think a certain piece of information is going to be elusive, you might consider searching for it at several different search sites to make the most of these differences, but there's an even better option: use a **meta search engine** such as MetaCrawler (Figure 7.4). Although you use this site in exactly the same way as AltaVista, mentioned above, it will simultaneously search over a dozen major search engines for you and return the results from each engine gathered together on a single page.

Sometimes a perfectly innocuous search can lead to search results containing links to 'adult' Web sites which you wouldn't want your children to see. To avoid this, there's a family-friendly search engine at ***http://www.mirago.co.uk/zone****, UK Plus at* ***http://www.ukplus.co.uk*** *aims to be family-friendly, and the other search engines are starting to provide options to filter out 'adult' links from searches. If you have children, you can point them to* ***http://www.yahooligans.com****, a safe and friendly search site providing links to sites for (or by) children.*

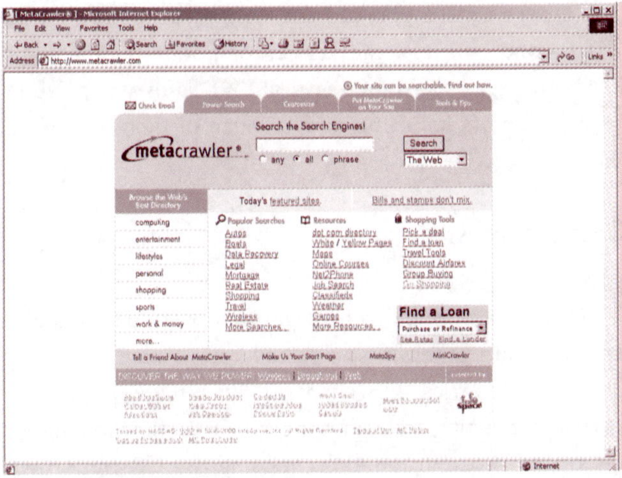

Figure 7.4

Speed up your searching with MetaCrawler!

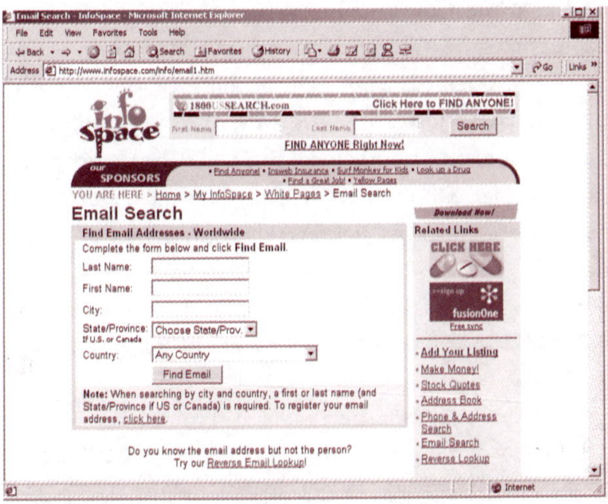

Figure 7.5

InfoSpace is the best choice for finding someone's e-mail address.

InfoSpace – Finding people

http://www.infospace.com/info/e-mail1.htm

http://www.infospace.com/info/people.htm

Finding people's e-mail addresses and other details isn't an exact science: just as there's no central repository of Web sites, there isn't the Internet equivalent of a telephone directory either. However, many companies have had a brave stab at creating something similar, and InfoSpace has done the best job (Figure 7.5). The first of the URLs above leads to a page where you can search for someone's e-mail address; at the second URL you can search for phone numbers and addresses. On both pages you'll find several text fields where you'll have to enter the person's full name, and as much of their address as you're able to.

Yell.com – Finding businesses

http://uk.yell.com

Just as there are search engines to help you find Web pages and e-mail addresses, there are others that can lead you to companies. The best of the lot is Yell.com at (not surprisingly) http://www.yell.com. When you arrive at the site you can choose between searching for US businesses or for those in the UK; choosing the UK option will lead you to the URL above (Figure 7.6).

This site is a lot like the Yellow Pages phone directory: if you know the name of the business you want to find, type it into the second text box, otherwise just enter the *type* of business into the first box. Type the town or county into the third box and press **Enter**. The search results will list all the likely matches, along with contact details and, in many cases, links to the company's Web site and a map of the area.

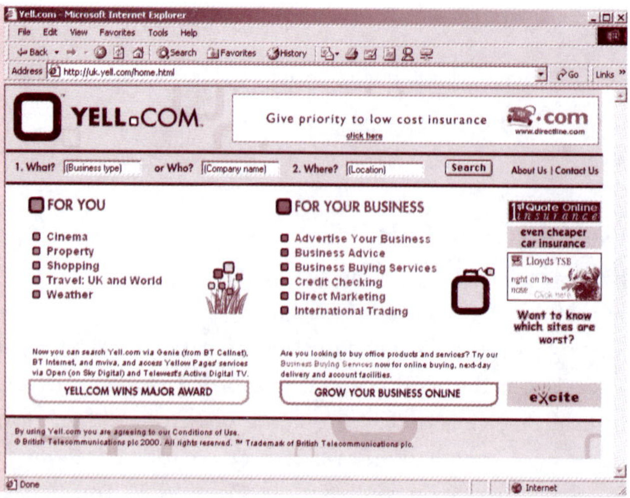

Figure 7.6

Search for British or American businesses at Yell.com.

Chatting on the Internet

On the Internet, 'chatting' doesn't involve using your voice at all. Instead you hold live conversations with others by typing on your keyboard. You type a line of text into a text field and press **Enter**, and the text is visible almost instantly to everyone else taking part. They can then respond by typing their own messages, and you'll see their responses on your screen.

Chatting brings you into the closest possible contact with other Internet users, and after talking to them for a while it's easy to forget that you really know nothing about them but what they've told you (which may not be true!). Never, ever, give out personal details such as addresses, phone numbers, passwords, credit card numbers, or school/college location when chatting.

Chatting usually takes place in a **chat room**, and the room may contain just a couple of people or it may contain several dozen. Fortunately, many of the room's occupants are only 'listening' to the conversation rather than actively taking part. Nevertheless, even with just half a dozen people chatting, things can get rather confused: sometimes nothing happens at all for a minute or so; at other times, everyone is talking at once and it's hard to tell who's talking to who!

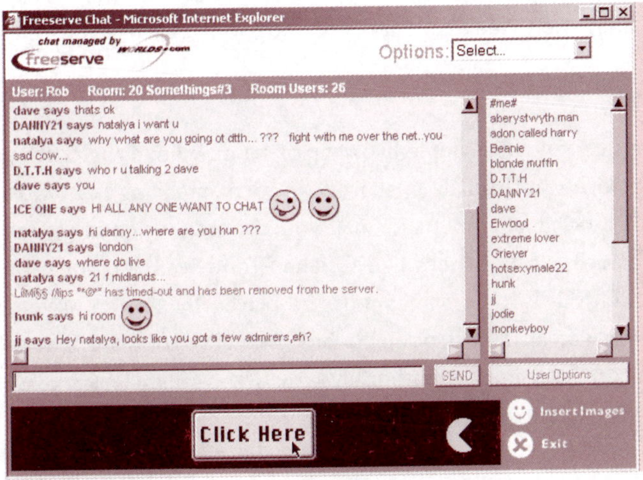

Figure 7.7

Typical chat in the Freeserve chat rooms.

The best way to get a taste of chatting is to visit the Freeserve chat site at http://www.freeserve.com/chat. When you arrive you'll be able to choose from a list of over a dozen different chat rooms: the name of each room is designed to attract people of different age groups or interests, so you'll have a rough idea what type of conversation to expect in each room by its name. Pick a room and type a nickname that you want to be known by while chatting, and a window like the one shown in Figure 7.7 will open.

*One of the most common uses for chat is to meet members of the opposite sex, and at some chat sites the conversation may not be suitable for children. AOL has its own **moderated** chat rooms (where a member of the service is keeping an eye on things to keep everything friendly) which are available to AOL members only, and these are a better bet for children.*

Network games

Games are the most widespread of human passions. From the tiny Gameboys to sophisticated consoles like Sega or Nintendo (not forgetting the traditional computer games), everyone can find a game to suit their tastes and finances. Thanks to the Internet, you can now pit your wits against contestants from all over the world, gamble real money, win real money and (needless to say) lose some very real money.

Games sites

Some games only need a simple browser or to download the correct software beforehand (usually in shareware form, meaning that you'll have to pay a nominal amount for it if you continue using it beyond its trial period), while others like Quake 2 and Total Annihilation require a CD-ROM. Some games must be played by several players, which is why 'virtual games rooms' (which, like chat rooms, are actually Web sites) have been created. Try http://www. gamesdomain. co.uk, http://www.ten.net and http://www.planetquake.com.

Role-playing games

Besides the games made popular by specialised software, you can get involved in role-playing games – terrifying medieval sagas, space-based stories or operatic dramas, and so on, among which the famous MUD (Multi User Dungeon) is without doubt the most popular. To try some of these games, go to http://www.thardferr.com or http://www.ssionline.com, or take a look at the rec.games.mud newsgroup.

Chess games

Finally, on a more intellectual note, how about a game of online chess from a specialised chess server? Go to http://www.chessclub.com to take part. (It's a good idea to choose a partner of the same ranking as you!)

8

HTML and Web site design

- The language of the Web
- What you need to write Web pages
- Getting started with Web design

In earlier chapters you've learnt how to use all the important areas of the Internet, but it's still *everyone else's* Internet you're using! Sooner or later you'll want to grab a little corner of it and make it your own. The mechanics of creating a Web site are simple enough, and in this chapter you'll learn how to do it. Of course, whole books have been written on this subject so this isn't an exhaustive reference, but it should get you off to a flying start. There are many guides and tutorials on the Web itself which can help you improve your skills, and you'll find two of the best at:

- http://werbach.com/barebones
- http://hotwired.lycos.com/webmonkey

The language of the Web

Pages on the World Wide Web are written in a language called **HTML** (HyperText Markup Language). The hypertext part is straightforward enough, we've met hypertext already – those underlined, clickable links that make the Web so easy to navigate. A *markup language* is a set of codes or signs added to plain text to indicate how it should be presented to the reader, noting bold or italic text, typefaces to be used, paragraph breaks, and so on. When you type any document into your word-processor, it adds these codes for you, but tactfully hides them from view: if you wanted bold text, for example, it *shows* you bold text instead of those codes. In HTML, however, you have to type in the codes yourself along with the text, and your browser puts the whole lot together before displaying it.

These codes are known as **tags**, and they consist of ordinary text placed between less-than and greater-than signs. Let's take an example:

```
<B>Welcome to my home page.</B> Glad you
could make it!
```

The first tag, `<B>`, means 'turn on bold type'. Halfway through the line, the same tag is used again, but with a forward-slash inserted straight after the less-than sign: this means 'turn off bold type'. If you displayed a page containing this line in your browser, it would look like this:

Welcome to my home page. Glad you could make it!

Of course, there's more to a Web page than bold text, so clearly there must be many more of these tags. But don't let that worry you – you don't have to learn all of them! There's a small bundle that you'll use a lot, and you'll get to know those very quickly. The rest will begin to sink in once you've used them a few times.

What you need to write Web pages

Believe it or not, creating a Web site is something you can do for free. Because HTML is entirely text-based, you can write your pages in Windows' Notepad, and we'll assume that's what you're doing. But there are other options, so let's quickly run through them.

WYSIWYG editors

In theory, WYSIWYG editors are the perfect way of working: instead of looking at plain text with HTML tags dotted around it, you see your Web page itself gradually taking shape, with images, colours and formatting displayed. There are a couple of drawbacks, though. First, WYSIWYG editors cost serious money compared with most other types of Internet software. Second, they probably won't help you to avoid learning something about HTML. Once in a while the editor won't do what you want it to do, and you'll have to switch to its text-editing mode to juggle the tags yourself.

> **+info**
>
> *WYSIWYG (pronounced 'wizzywig') is an acronym for 'What you see is what you get'. This is used to describe many different types of software that can show you on the screen exactly what something will look like when you print it on paper or view it in your Web browser.*

You might even find that it's far easier to learn the language itself than it is to learn how the WYSIWYG software works, but if you'd like to give the WYSIWYG method a shot, here are three of the most popular programs:

- **Microsoft FrontPage**. You can find out more about this at http://www. microsoft.com/frontpage, but you'll have to take a trip into town to buy a copy. (FrontPage is also included with Microsoft Office Premium edition.)
- **Microsoft FrontPage Express**. A cut-down version of FrontPage included with recent editions of Windows and Internet Explorer.
- **NetObjects Fusion**. A stylish program with a huge number of high-quality page templates, available from http://www.netobjects.com.

Markup editors

Using a markup editor is rather like using Notepad – you see all the HTML code on the page in front of you. But instead of having to type in tags yourself, a markup editor will insert them for you at the click of a button or the press of a hotkey, in the same way that you use your word-processor (Figure 8.1). You might still choose to type in some of the simple tags yourself, such as the tag for bold text mentioned earlier, but for more complicated elements such as a table with a lot of cells, this automation is a great time and sanity saver.

Markup editors are also ideal for newcomers to HTML. If you don't know one tag from another, just click the appropriate buttons on the toolbar to insert them: once you've seen them appear on the page a few times, you'll soon start to remember what's what!

Here are three of the most popular and feature-packed markup editors. You'll need to register these if you want to use them beyond the trial period.

- **HomeSite** from http://www.allaire.com
- **HoTMetaL Pro** from http://www.sq.com
- **HTMLed** from http://www.ist.ca

Text converters

Some modern word-processors like Lotus WordPro and Microsoft Word have begun to include features to turn your documents into Web pages. At their simplest, they'll let you create an ordinary word-processed document and then choose a **Save as HTML**

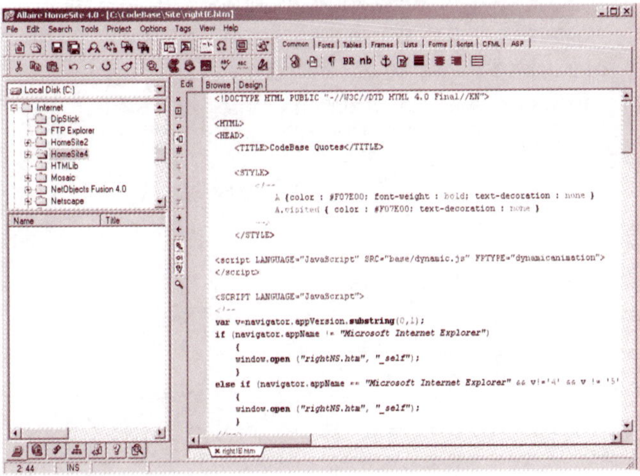

Figure 8.1

Colour-coding and one-click tag insertion in HomeSite.

option from the **File** menu to convert it into a Web page. The result won't be as effective as other pages on the Web, but it's an ideal way to convert a long document when the only other option is to add all the tags yourself!

+info

If you use Microsoft Office, the Web authoring features don't stop at Word. Excel allows you to save a worksheet in HTML format, and PowerPoint helps you create multimedia pages by converting slides to Web format. You'll also find a media library of pictures, sounds and animations that you can include in your pages, however you choose to create them.

You can also create Web pages from scratch in these programs. For example, Microsoft Word has its own Web Page Wizard that can set you up with a ready-to-edit template. To start it up, go to **File/New...**, then click the **Web Pages** tab and double-click **Web Page Wizard**. You can add and delete elements on the page, and use the standard drawing and editing toolbars to slot in anything else you need.

Getting started with Web design

Start Notepad, and type the text below (without worrying about the exact number of spaces or carriage returns). Save this file using any name you like, but make sure you give it the extension **.htm** or **.html**. Every Web page you write must be saved with one of these extensions – it doesn't matter which you choose, but you'll find life a lot easier if you stick to the same one each time!

```
<!DOCTYPE HTML PUBLIC "-//W3C//DTD HTML
4.0//EN">

<HTML>
<HEAD>
    <TITLE>Untitled</TITLE>
</HEAD>

<BODY>


</BODY>
</HTML>
```

None of those tags does anything exciting by itself, but it's worth knowing what they're all for. The first line is a piece of technical nonsense that tells a browser that the document is written in the latest version of the HTML language. The rest of the document is placed between the `<HTML>` and `</HTML>` tags, and falls into two separate chunks: the **head** (the section between `<HEAD>` and `</HEAD>`) and the **body** (between `<BODY>` and `</BODY>`).

The document's head is pretty dull: all it contains is the title of the document, inserted between the `<TITLE>` and `</TITLE>` tags. There are other bits and pieces that can be slotted in here, but the title is the only element that *must* be included.

The body section is the one that matters. Between these two tags you'll type all the text that should appear on your page, and put in the tags you need to display images, set colours, insert hyperlinks to other pages and sites, and anything else you want your page to contain.

Now that you've created a basic template, let's add some text and formatting to it to build up a Web page.

+info

Although we've used capital letters for the tags in these examples, you don't have to do the same. But typing tags in capitals makes them stand out from the rest of your text, which can be useful for editing.

Page title and text

The first thing to do is to replace the word **Untitled** with a sensible title for the document, such as **Links To The Best Multimedia Sites** or **My EastEnders Home Page**. Pick something that describes what the page will be about, but keep it fairly short: the text between the `<TITLE>` and `</TITLE>` tags will appear in the title-bar at the very top of most browsers, and if your entry is too long to fit it'll just get chopped off!

Now we'll add some text to the page. Either type the same text as in the example below, or replace the first and second paragraph entries with whole paragraphs if you prefer. When you've done that, save the file as **links.html**, but don't close Notepad yet.

```
<!DOCTYPE HTML PUBLIC "-//W3C//DTD HTML
4.0//EN">

<HTML>
<HEAD>
   <TITLE>Links To The Best Multimedia
   Sites</TITLE>
</HEAD>

<BODY>
<H1>Welcome To My Home page!</H1>
Here's the first paragraph.
<P>And here's the second paragraph.

</BODY>
</HTML>
```

Now take a look at your masterpiece in your browser. There are several ways you can do this: find the file you just saved and double-click it, or open your browser and type the path to the file in the address bar, or choose **File/Open** and click on **Browse**. When your browser displays it, it should look just like Figure 8.2.

So what are those new tags all about? Let's take the <P> tag first. This tells your browser to present the following text as a new paragraph, which automatically inserts a blank line before it. And this raises an important point about HTML: you can't insert blank lines

Figure 8.2

A simple home page.

just by pressing the **Enter** key. Although *you* can see blank lines in Notepad when you do that, your browser will just ignore them, which is why you need to start a new paragraph by entering <P>. (Notice that you don't have to put in a closing </P> at the end of a paragraph – the act of starting a new paragraph isn't an ongoing effect that has to be turned off again.)

> **+info**
>
> *Another tag, <BR>, will give you a 'line break' to let you start a new line without starting a new paragraph. In other words, the text that follows that tag will start at the beginning of the next line, with no empty line inserted before it.*

The other pair of tags that cropped up was <H1> and </H1> which formats a line of text as a heading. You can choose from six sizes: H1 is the largest, followed by <H2> and </H2> down to the smallest, <H6> and </H6>. In one nifty little manoeuvre, these tags change the size of the text you place between them *and* make it bold. They also automatically start a new paragraph for the heading (so you don't need to place a <P> tag at the start of the line) and start a new paragraph for whatever follows the heading. Try changing the size of the heading by altering those tags to see the different effects, re-saving the file, and clicking your browser's **Refresh** button to update it.

Formatting text

The tags for bold and italic text are easy to remember: <B> for bold, and <I> for italic. As both of these are ongoing effects, you'll have to enter closing tags (</B> or </I>) when you want the effect to stop. And, just as in your word-processor, you can combine these tags, so if your document contained this:

```
This is <I>italic</I>. This is <B>bold</B>.
This is <B><I>bold & italic</I></B>.
```

the result would look like this in your browser:

This is *italic*. This is **bold**. This is ***bold & italic***.

There are many other text tags, and of course you can add links to other sites, add background colours, images, and so on, but they are beyond the scope of this book. Now's the time to visit the two sites listed at the beginning of this chapter!

9

The Internet and multimedia

- **What do you need?**
- **Real Player**
- **MP3 audio**
- **Movies**
- **Shockwave animation**

One of the most important reasons for the surge in popularity of the Internet when the World Wide Web came along was the fact that the Web made the Internet fun to use. Not only was it possible to find information, it was possible to find entertainment in the form of music, sounds, video, interactivity and animation – a true multimedia experience. In this chapter we'll look at some of the multimedia elements used on the Web, and point you towards Web sites that will give you a taste of what's on offer.

What do you need?

Most of the software you need to enjoy the Web's multimedia offerings is free, and comes in the form of programs called **plug-ins**. A plug-in is a program that attaches itself to your browser (in a metaphorical rather than physical way!) during installation and waits invisibly in the background until you try to play the kind of multimedia file it was designed to handle.

There are hundreds of different plug-ins available, between them handling hundreds of different types of multimedia file. But the good news is that you don't need all those separate plug-ins: some of the best can handle many different types of media, so you probably won't need to install more than two or three extra programs to handle the majority of multimedia files you come across. And if you're using Windows Millennium or Internet Explorer v5.5 (or later versions of either of those) you may not need any new software at all. A Windows Media Player is included with both of these, which is capable of handling almost everything the Web can throw at it. You can download the Windows Media Player as a separate item from http://www.microsoft.com/windows/windowsmedia.

Real Player

You won't travel far on the Web before arriving at a site that uses RealAudio for music, speech, or a mixture of the two. RealAudio is a *streaming* format that plays as the file is being transferred, with none of that tedious waiting around for the sound file to download first. As soon as you click a RealAudio link, your Real Player opens (as shown in Figure 9.1), grabs the first few seconds of the transmission to help it to stay one jump ahead and ensure smooth playback, and then starts to play. You can pause or stop playback by clicking the appropriate buttons, or replay the entire clip from the beginning. If you have Internet Explorer you don't need to do anything more – the RealAudio plug-in is bundled with it. If you're using a different

> **+info**
>
> *RealAudio doesn't offer great sound quality – some sacrifices have to be made for the files to transfer this fast. Top-quality sound comes in the form of* ***.wav*** *files, which Internet Explorer can play without any extra help, and these weigh in at up to 10Mb for a top-quality one-minute file! Smaller* ***.mid*** *files use the sounds built into your soundcard, so quality of the results depends a lot on the quality of your card.*

browser, you'll have to visit http://www.real.com to download and install the player software.

Once you've installed the Real Player, as with all multimedia plug-ins, your first stop should be the Web site of the people who wrote the program – you'll always find plenty of samples and links to let you play with your new toy once you've installed it. In this case, then, go to http://www.real.com. A couple of other good sites are Virgin Radio at http://www.virginradio.co.uk and London's Capital Radio at http://www.capitalfm.com, where you can hear the live radio broadcasts while you surf.

MP3 audio

The MP3 format is a relatively new innovation that claims to pack near-CD-quality music into comparatively small files (a typical song weighs in at between 1Mb and 2Mb). Whether the quality is near enough to a CD to be listenable for long periods is a matter of taste,

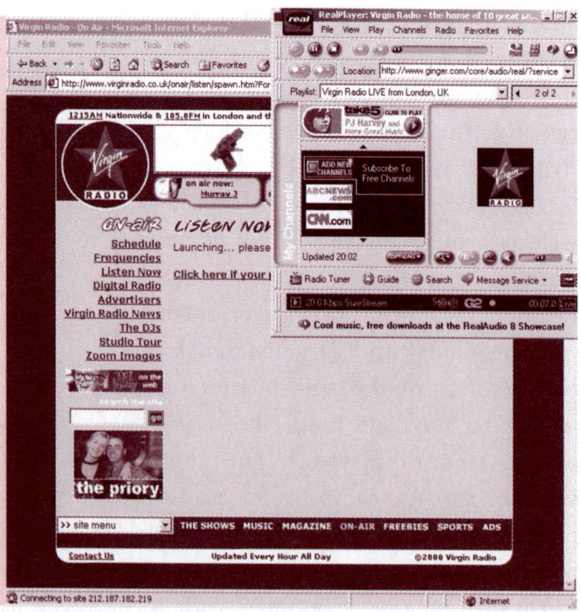

Figure 9.1

A live broadcast from Virgin Radio playing in Real Player.

Figure 9.2

The popular (and very stylish) Winamp MP3 player.

but these files have been the 'big thing' on the Net over the last couple of years and hundreds of Web sites have sprung up offering free MP3 music.

One of the most popular MP3 players is Winamp from http://www.winamp.com (shown in Figure 9.2) which can also play CDs and other audio formats. Both the Real Player and Windows Media Player also have MP3 playback capability. To try out the MP3 format for yourself, visit http://www.mp3.com, http://www.mp3now.com or http://www.mp3sound.com.

Movies

The first thing to be aware of here is that movie files are *big!* A one-minute movie will be roughly 2.5Mb, and in most cases you'll have to wait for the whole file to download before you can watch it. All the same, as with most multimedia elements, it pays to have the software installed just in case you come across something that really seems worth the wait!

The three most common types of movie file on the Web are MPEG (which will have **.mpeg**, **.mpg** or **.mpe** extensions), QuickTime (**.mov** or **.qt**), and Video For Windows (**.avi**). The Windows Media Player can handle these, but it occasionally has problems with the QuickTime format, so you might want to download the dedicated player from http://www.apple.com/quicktime.

Figure 9.3

Watch movie trailers at QuickTime's Web site.

Ready to watch some videos? To make the most of your QuickTime Player, head for http://www.apple.com/quicktime/hotpicks where you'll find links to movies, music and QuickTime virtual reality. Or visit QuickTime TV at http://www.apple.com/quicktime/qtv and pick a channel. To see trailers of the latest cinema releases (shown in Figure 9.3) go to http://www.apple.com/quicktime/trailers.

The MPEG format is used mostly for animations nowadays, and you can find a great collection at http://wwwzenger.informatik.tu-muenchen.de/persons/paula/mpeg.

Shockwave animation

The word *animation* doesn't sound cool, but it's a major multimedia craze on the Internet. Where images and text have always been fixed on the page, they can now move around and react to the mouse passing over them. Part of this popularity lies in the fact that animations are easier for the average user to create than videos, and they take no more time to download than an image.

The most common type of animation is ShockWave, which you can view in Internet Explorer without adding anything else to your software mountain. (If you're not using Internet Explorer, you'll have to visit http://www. macromedia.com to download the plug-in.) To find out what all the fuss is about, visit Macromedia's own Shockwave Gallery at http://www.shockwave.com (Figure 9.4), or play a few games at http://clevermedia.com/arcade.

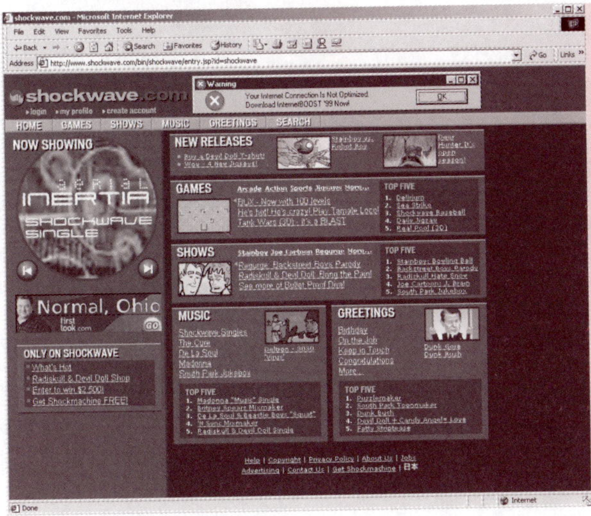

Figure 9.4

Animation really is better than you'd expect: find out at **www.shockwave.com**.

index